Grips

GRIPS

JUDO MASTERCLASS TECHNIQUES

NEIL ADAMS
with Eddie Ferrie

IPPON/CROWOOD

This edition published in 1992 by
Ippon Books
55 Long Lane,
London N3 2HY
England.

First published in 1990 by
The Crowood Press
Gipsy Lane, Swindon,
Wiltshire SN2 6DQ

British Library Cataloguing in Publication Data
Adams, Neil *1958–*
    Grips: masterclass techniques.
    1. Judo
    2. Title
    796.8'152

ISBN 09518455 6 X

Photographs by David Finch, Judo Photos Unlimited with extra contest
photographs by Eddie Ferrie.

Acknowledgements
Special thanks must go, as always, to David Finch for his expert
photographic work. John O'Brien and the High Wycombe Judo Club
generously loaned the dojo for the photo session. Eddie Ferrie helped
me to put the whole book together and I would not have finished it on
time without his help.

Set in 10 on 11½pt Optima Light

Typeset by Avonset, Midsomer Norton, Bath
Printed in Great Britain by Dotesios Ltd, Trowbridge, Wiltshire.

Contents

Foreword

Anton Geesink, the Dutch Olympic and World Champion, once reduced the complex skill of gripping to two simple concepts. He called the sleeve grip 'the working hand' and the lapel grip 'the playing hand'.

Kisaburo Watanabe and Trevor Leggett, in their classic analysis of *tai-otoshi*, used a different image. They called the sleeve grip 'the long pull' and the lapel grip 'the short pull'.

Both are useful in their contexts. But the truth is that grips is an immense subject that cannot be encapsulated in conveniently brief catch-phrases.

The traditional Japanese view looks at grips in terms of *hikite* (the main pull, which is generally the sleeve grip) and *tsurite* (the drawing hand, which is generally the lapel grip). Typically, the words carry their own special image which mirrors the action: *tsurite*, for example, comes from the Japanese word *tsuri*, to fish, and incorporates the idea of drawing an opponent off balance, just as a fishing rod bends when it draws a fish out of the water.

The modern view of unorthodox attacks typified by the Russian style approaches grips in a very different way. Anything within the rules has become not just acceptable but almost the norm, and there is now a bewildering array of attacking grips, defensive grips and tactical grips in use.

Anyone who has practised with Neil Adams, or seen him in competition or *randori*, knows that he has an extensive understanding of grips. Trying to get a grip on him is no small undertaking, though he always seems to be able to get the grip he wants.

While he generally favoured a traditional sleeve/lapel grip himself during the height of his competition days, he was able to adapt to the different grips as circumstances demanded. And because he faced top fighters with so many different styles, he was aware of the effectiveness, the limitations and the dangers of the panoply of grips.

In this book, he has outlined some of the basic principles of the main gripping skills. He does not pretend that it is a definitive book on grips because, with the wide range of existing throwing techniques, such a thing is probably impossible within a one-volume format.

His aim is to make judoka more aware of the subtleties and implications of particular grips, and of what can be done with the hands in a creative manner to produce the spectacular throws that are at the heart of judo.

He firmly believes that a greater understanding of grips can make a dramatic difference to everyone's judo, for no matter how fast an entry into a throw, or how strong an attack, if the grips are not correct the throw will simply not work.

A book of this kind has never been attempted – not even in Japan. But we think that the experiment has proved worthwhile, and that *Grips* will enrich everyone's judo knowledge and judo practice.

Nicolas Soames
Masterclass Series Editor

Grips: A Personal View

In 1977 a young Englishman, just eighteen years of age, stepped on to the mat to fight one of the greatest judo players of all time, the World and Olympic Light Middleweight Champion at the time, Vladimir Nevzerov of the Soviet Union. The young Englishman was me and the event was the European Senior Championships in Ludwigshafen, West Germany.

In the photograph taken of that first encounter you can see a young Neil Adams wearing a judogi that looks at least two sizes too big compared with the tailored fit of the suit worn by the World Champion. The photograph places the young pretender, with everything to learn, in dramatic counterpoint to the seasoned champion Nevzerov, who that day was to quell the young tornado and give him a lesson he would never forget.

At this stage in my judo career, I had not really considered the importance of gripping or its complexities in any real depth, but there I was exchanging grips with a master and doing what to a degree came naturally to me. Even without much expertise in *kumikata* I was able to neutralise much of Nevzerov's onslaught and finished the contest with only a *koka* scored against me. I can explain my relative success only in terms of instinctive reflexes, just as when someone throws a punch at your head and you move out of the way or get hit. I had survived through some innate and spontaneous quality rather than any learned skill. Although I lost to Nevzerov it had been a learning experience.

Immediately afterwards I went out and bought a judogi that fitted, and for the first time began a serious in-depth study of *kumikata*. I wanted to know why I had been unable to grip my opponent and how I should ensure that I would be able to do so when we next met. I had to learn what else was required other than making instinctive reflex

Fig 1 Youth versus experience. From the 1977 European Championships in Ludwigshafen: myself aged 18, in combat with the reigning World and Olympic champion, Vladimir Nevzerov of the Soviet Union.

actions to combat his superior gripping skills. This was the beginning of a study which has continued until the present day and I cannot overemphasise the importance of skill in *kumikata* for success in judo.

My many trips to Japan reinforced my belief in its importance. Some of the Japanese I practised with were so good at gripping it was virtually impossible to make an effective attack – as a result they could perform their techniques virtually unimpeded. Nishida – who I unexpectedly threw for ippon in the Kano Cup with *uchimata* – was one such expert at grips that springs to mind. Although he was never World or Olympic Champion I honestly believe that for a three-year period he was easily the best under-71kg player in the world; whenever we did *randori* he could knock me down at will. Obviously this was an intolerable situation from my point of view and one that had to change.

On my first trip to Japan, just a boy and aged only sixteen I had stepped on to a mat full of black belts. It was just a routine training session, but I was thrilled and excited by the prospect of being able to practise with many high-grade partners. The excitement soon turned to

frustration, however, and after about two hours of being thrown from one end of the dojo to the other I was close to tears. Their superiority was entirely attributable to their better gripping skills. After about four days things began to change for me as I adapted and began to grasp how they were able to frustrate me, and I then began using some of their own techniques on them.

The big problem in the early years was always strength in the hands, wrists and forearms, and I had to do a lot of specialist strengthening work. It was amazing how quickly the forearms would pump up with blood and lactic acid, making gripping so painful that it became unbearable, but over time my young boy's hands changed form, becoming strong, highly specialised pieces of equipment. My knuckle joints enlarged to cope with the extra stress put on them, as did my wrists and forearms, and my stamina improved. Eventually I found I could at last compete on an equal basis with the best in the world and could concentrate on improving my technique in conjunction with my gripping skills. I firmly believe that everyone can improve their *kumikata* and, although natural aptitude and talent help, technical study and knowledge gleaned from experience make a huge contribution.

To this day I remain a judoka who prefers to stand up straight and do traditional upright judo, which has probably lost me some contests in my career. I have never liked the grovelling style of judo that is sometimes forced upon us as a result of modern tactical grip play, which has nothing to offer the sport as I want to know it. I remember my European final in 1983 against Fogarasi of Hungary being marred by such tactics.

Fogarasi had simply decided to get through the contest without being thrown. There was no exchange of techniques, no spirited battle of wills and skills. That day, he opted just to negate every positive move I tried to make and made none himself. In my opinion it was a disgraceful performance. He had shown himself to be very able throughout the day, winning a number of contests by ippon and throwing the Russian in the semifinal. The final, though, was a débâcle. Fogarasi's tactics were to prevent me from taking any kind of usable grip. After the full five minutes had elapsed he had been penalised up to *keikoku* and I won the contest, but I felt that he should have been disqualified. The following day my feeling was endorsed by the referee's commission, which on reflection decided that he should have been disqualified after three minutes rather than five, as such extreme negativity was against the spirit of judo.

At the other end of the scale there are the positive grippers, those who you know are going to throw you if they get their grips. Yasuhiro Yamashita, probably the greatest judo champion of all time, trained in England for one year and we had many randoris together at The Budokwai in London. In spite of the obvious difference in our weights, I never felt in any danger of injury when we trained together. His skill was such that when you were thrown by him it was always clean and crisp, although a little hard at times. Yamashita's grip was the traditional sleeve lapel, which I feel is more suitable for heavyweights because their judo tends to be more static than that of the lighter weights. Having said that, Yamashita's entry for his

Fig 2   Khabarelli, the master of the unorthodox grip and attack. The right hand has gripped the belt over the shoulder, the left has caught the trouser leg. The initial ouchi-gari *attack has been redirected into a sort of lifting knee whirlspin and his opponent does not know what is happening; there is no Japanese name for this technique!*

Fig 3 Yasuhiro Yamashita's ouchi-gari. *The left hand or* tsurite *is pinning his partner's weight on the leg which is under attack. The right hand or* hikite *pulls on the sleeve, spreading the opponent's arms and driving his weight down into the mat.*

techniques was as quick and as deft as any lightweight's in the world. I remember that the first time we practised together I was determined to do positive judo and not resort to tactical gripping, which is against my natural instincts. Unhappily, I soon discovered that this was the only way to avoid being thrown. Every time Yamashita managed to get his favourite grip he inevitably threw me, usually for ippon.

One night I decided I had had enough of this and resolved to keep my left sleeve as far away from him as possible. I was determined not to be thrown, and I fought him as though in a contest and not a practice session. As his frustration increased he began to change into a higher gear himself, and I was attacked with at least ten powerful techniques, only the relatively small size of the crowded dojo preventing him from finishing. Yamashita's hopping *uchimata* and *ouchi-gari* attacks took us from one end of The Budokwai to the other. I hit the wall with such force and speed that I remember thinking that something had to be done to get out of a situation that was rapidly turning into a nightmare.

Luckily for me, I was running the session and a breathless shout of 'change partners', just before he launched another hopping *osoto-gari* attack, saved me from further bouncing off the wall. Yamashita, who was just getting into his stride, did not really understand the mentality behind such an action, although certain members of the club were obviously amused by it. He was clearly intrigued by the experience, though, because he asked me for a second and a third practice. I concluded that it would have been easier to have adopted my normal, traditional style of judo from the beginning, instead of the kind of Fogarasi tactics to which I am so opposed. Yamashita and myself are good friends, of course, and towards the end of his stay in England he grew more accustomed to the British sense of humour – luckily for me!

In complete contrast to Yamashita's traditional style of gripping, the most unorthodox fighting style of anyone I ever met in contest was that of Shota Khabarelli of the Soviet Union. Khabarelli was a brilliant fighter, the Olympic Champion in 1980, with a style unique even among the unorthodox Russians. He favoured a grip over the top of his opponent's shoulders, securing the belt before attacking with a variety of combinable throws, mongrel forms of *uranage harai-makikomi* and *ouchi-gari*. In all our battles I was never able to settle into my own rhythm of gripping and attacking; the feeling was of a fight for survival lasting for the duration of the contest. This normally resulted in the need to adopt an extreme jigotai and for 100 per cent concentration on neutralising his grips, which was the only way to beat him.

For me, Yamashita and Khabarelli epitomise the traditional and the unorthodox. Though worlds apart in style and approach, they were nevertheless both able to become Olympic Champions by operating their own particular styles of judo from their own grips. Both men represent an ideal in seeking the ippon throw, which is what I feel everyone should be looking for in their judo – whether a Yamashita, a Khabarelli, or even a Fogarasi. Of course, it is not always possible to do textbook classic judo against awkward opponents, and sometimes other methods must be adopted. But for judo to continue to evolve in a positive way, we have to ensure that the traditional, fast, dynamic techniques are complemented, not ruined, by developments in *kumikata*.

Judo is anything but predictable. I was very surprised when, shortly after the Seoul Olympics, a highly respected Japanese coach, and former World Champion, said that he thought it would be very difficult, if not impossible, to produce a book which provided a detailed study of gripping for judo. This detailed study is my own contribution to the future development of *kumikata* and is the result of asking myself a simple question many years ago: why are Japanese judoka superior in their gripping and what must we do to improve our own skills?

A History of Grips

Judo has been described as a sport, an act of self-defence, a form of physical training and even a way of life. It is all of these things and more for many different people, but in essence judo is a form of wrestling. Like other forms of wrestling, judo involves fighting standing up, where the aim is to throw the opponent to the ground, and ground fighting or grappling, where the objective is to pin, armlock or strangle the opponent into submission. What distinguishes judo from other forms of wrestling is the judogi, the judo uniform which consists of a jacket, trousers and a belt. This uniform provides for the possibility of virtually open-ended skill acquisition and the use of a range and variety of fighting skills unparalleled in any other sport.

The judogi is fundamentally a training suit based on the traditional Japanese kimono, woven strong enough to withstand the stresses and strains of gripping and pulling. Judo was

conceived both as a martial art and a sport, and it is logical from the point of view of self-defence to expect an attacker to be wearing clothes. The use of the judogi in practice is as important to the judo player as the bamboo sword or shinai is to the kendoka.

Of course in Europe we have always understood the basic importance of gripping – at the very least you have to grip to throw. But in the early days, we failed to realise that it was generally the superiority of Japanese fighters in gripping that made them so much stronger and more effective in both practice and competition.

The reasons for the superiority of Japanese fighters' *kumikata* are quite straightforward. Judo has existed in Japan as a part of the Japanese educational system since before the turn of the century. Literally millions of Japanese have donned judogi and stepped on the mats to practise and compete. Thousands

Figs 4–6 *Adaptive gripping at the highest level is virtually instinctive and is often born of desperation. In this example from the 1975 World Championships in Vienna, Chochoshvilli of the Soviet Union attacks Uemura of Japan, who is fighting from an extreme left stance, with an immensely powerful harai-tsuri-komi-ashi.*

Fig 5 *The Japanese fighter is thrown, but has begun his counter-attack in mid-air, grabbing the Russian's leg with his right hand.*

Fig 6 *By keeping this grip and going with the force of the throw the Japanese avoided being thrown for ippon and conceded only a waza-ari. He was then able to turn the Russian, who banged his head on the mat and was momentarily dazed, and hold him for ippon.*

of these have in turn become expert and have passed on their skills to subsequent generations, creating a very broad skill base. Judo was compulsory in high school in Japan and even now there are about a million people practising on any given day. The sheer volume of people doing judo means that there are a lot of very good fighters and quite a few really excellent ones.

Twenty years ago the number of people practising judo in many European countries could be counted in hundreds, and it is therefore hardly surprising that Japanese judo was for so long so far in advance of the rest of the world, both technically and in terms of the physical preparation undertaken by their top competitors. Their physical dominance was a result not simply of greater power, but of a knowledge of how to apply it and to negate an opponent through skilful gripping.

When Yukio Tani came to England in 1899, the level of organised competitive judo in Japan was already very high. Upon arriving in England he was able to go around the music halls challenging all-comers to don the unfamiliar judo jacket, and could then exploit their lack of familiarity with it. The myth of Japanese invincibility began with Tani. In fact he was never defeated by a foreigner; many of those he fought, even the skilled wrestlers and boxers, had never even seen many of the numerous throws, strangles and armlocks he used to subdue them.

Fig 7   This modern-style grip is taken from an illustration from a collection of self-defence moves presented in a series of engravings by the seventeenth-century Dutch engraver, Romeyn de Hoogue, and based on the instructions of an early Dutch traveller to Japan.

The year 1918 was a landmark in the history of judo in Britain, seeing the founding of the first club in Europe, The Budokwai in London, by the Japanese-born Gunji Koizumi. British judo proper began in 1948 with the founding of the British Judo Association, and the first World Championships were held in 1956, the Japanese reigning supreme, taking the gold medals in all three categories.

Many non-Japanese fighters in the early days began to feel that they were competing against a race which produced individuals of superhuman proportions, although we now know that this was not the case. One consequence of this notion of Japanese invincibility was that a number of top judo players from the West went to Japan to train and learn from the inventors of the sport. Many good judo men fell into the trap of staying in Japan too long

and trying to train exactly like the Japanese. Some of them were sidetracked by the distractions of life in Tokyo, but there is little doubt that a number of these British fighters were potential World Champions who did their best judo in Japanese dojos but then failed to realise their true potential in World and Olympic competition, where it was necessary to revert to the less rhythmical, more physical European style. One European who got the balance right, dividing his time between training in Japan and competing in Europe, was the giant Dutchman, Anton Geesink.

Geesink was the man who made judo a truly international sport by defeating the Japanese champion Sone in the 3rd World Championships in Paris in 1961, becoming the first non-Japanese in history to become a World Champion at judo. Superior *kumikata* was an important factor in Geesink's victory because, as well as being much bigger,

Fig 8   In a spirited account of The Fine Art of Ju-Jitsu, *published in 1906, Mrs Watts opened up the possibilities of practising the martial arts to women as well as men.*

heavier and stronger (through systematic weight training) than his Japanese opponent, he was also extremely skilful. Whenever Sone tried to get his grip, Geesink simply tore free, completely dominating the Japanese before bowling him over with a powerful *soto-makikomi* and holding him down.

Geesink's victory had a profound effect on Japanese judo, and some of Japan's top competitors, including Isao Inokuma, began weight training as a direct result of it. They recognised that, for all their skill, they would be no match for Geesink in the forthcoming Olympic games in Tokyo if they did not. Inokuma collaborated with American Don Draeger and went on to win the first Olympic heavyweight title in Tokyo in 1964. Geesink, though, had opted to fight openweight and, in defeating the All-Japan champion Akio Kaminaga in the final, with a skilful *sasae-tsuri-komi ashi* and hold down, he shattered the myth of Japanese supremacy for ever.

After Geesink, the next great shock for the Japanese and everyone else was the arrival of the Russians on the international scene. With a strong tradition already established in sombo wrestling, but no hope of Olympic recognition for that sport, the Russians turned to judo in a big way, wreaking havoc upon the rest of the world with their unorthodox gripping, throwing and armlocking methods. They appeared as different from traditional Japanese-style judo as a cavalry sabre is from a katana, but proved to be just as effective. The Russians were content to grip any part of the judogi including the trousers and belt, and were particularly adept at pick-ups and sacrifice techniques from unexpected situations.

In the first ever match between the two countries, the Russians defeated the Japanese and made it clear that judo was no longer exclusively their property. The Japanese team were all fifth dans and included some very well known names such as Endo and Uemura. The Russians, who perhaps have their own particular sense of humour, were all heavyweight first dans at the time, but some names such as Chochoshvilli and Novikov were soon to become renowned in the judo world.

It came as a surprise to everyone that such unorthodox grips could be so effective and that training methods would have to evolve to take them into consideration. Their tradition in sombo (which is similar to judo although it has a different look and feel) gave the Russians a head start over most of Europe and it still stands them in good stead today.

Another big Dutchman named Wilhelm Ruska had followed in the footsteps of his countryman Geesink, winning World heavyweight title in 1967 and 1971, and the gold medal at both heavyweight and open in the 1972 Munich Olympic games. It was not until the mid-seventies, however, that Japanese supremacy in the lighter weights began to crumble. After winning gold medals in every category in the World Championships in Lausanne in Switzerland in 1973, Japanese judo had seemed to be invincible once again – at the very next World Championships though, this trend was reversed, with the Russians Nevzerov and Dvoinikov taking the gold and silver respectively at light middleweight, a category the Japanese had never been defeated in. The light heavyweight title was taken by the formidable Jean-Luc Rouge of France.

This trend towards a sharing out of medals continued through the seventies and early eighties with World Champions emerging from other countries such as East Germany, South Korea and Great Britain, while countries such as Italy, Cuba, Belgium and Switzerland produced their own Olympic Champions in Gamba, Rodriguez, Van de Valle and Rothlisberger. All of these emerging champions were the product of combining traditional and modern methods of skill and conditioning training.

In the early eighties still more 'new' coun-

15

tries took their share of Olympic gold medals, with Peter Seisenbacher of Austria and Frank Wienecke of West Germany making the Los Angeles judo event a teutonic treat.

The South Koreans, in particular, began to approach judo professionally in preparation for the 1988 Olympics, incorporating full-time training for their national squad members and making great use of weights to get as strong as possible. This approach paid off, with Korean fighters taking gold medals in the under-60kg and under-65kg categories. Korean fighters are currently among the hardest to fight because they combine the technical and gripping skills of the typical Japanese with the strength and condition of the top Western fighters.

The 1988 Olympic games were a landmark in the history of world judo, with every category except the heavyweight being won by a non-Japanese. Judo has rapidly developed from being the domain of one or two countries into a truly world-wide international sport. Fourteen different countries shared twenty-eight medals.

One category especially illustrated the importance of *kumikata*. The brilliant Japanese technician Hitoshi Sugai had been favourite for the Olympic gold under-95kg category prior to the event. Sugai was a perfect example of a classical fighter who had developed extra gripping skills to become World Champion in Seoul three years earlier. He had thrown all his opponents for ippon with left *uchimata* to reach the final and, under extreme pressure from the Korean Olympic Champion Hyoung-Zoo Ha, he had switched totally unexpectedly from a left grip to a right-handed grip, throwing the Korean for ippon with right *tai-otoshi* in the dying seconds.

His left *uchimata* again won him a second World title in Essen in 1987. It was well known to be so sharp that none of his opponents wanted to let him grip with his right hand anywhere, let alone on the left sleeve. Whenever he got his right hand on he invariably scored ippon. Such was the extent of Sugai's gripping skills that he developed the ability to throw for ippon with *uchimata* with just a grip on his opponent's wrist. In the final against Meyer of Holland he was unable to get a grip with his right hand, such was Meyer's extreme posture and determination. But even so he twice swept away the Dutchman's leading leg with *ashiwaza*, scoring *yuko*, with only his left hand on Meyer's right lapel.

Yet, despite his undoubted brilliance, in the Seoul Olympics Sugai lost his first contest to an awkward, lanky, long-armed French fighter, Stephane Traineau, who simply messed up the Japanese fighter's rhythm and prevented him from taking his favourite end-of-sleeve grip. Traineau in turn lost to Aurelio Miguel of Brazil, who went on to become the first Olympic Champion ever to win his gold medal without throwing, holding, armlocking or strangling any of his opponents by ippon. He won every fight in the under-95kg category on decisions, outgripping his opponents and beating them to the attack, getting them penalised for passivity, but not actually scoring. The ultimate reward in the sport of judo was won by a superbly fit athlete who had shown real judo skill only in his grip fighting. The grip in this event, as so often before, had made the difference between an early shower and the gold medal.

Grip and Attack:
Orthodox Methods

This chapter deals with what should be the main function of any grip: throwing the opponent for ippon. It covers general principles of gripping and considers the notion of appropriateness, specifically applied to the orthodox classical sleeve lapel grip.

The Function of Grips

The grip must fulfil three requirements: set the opponent up to be thrown (*kuzushi* or balance breaking); allow you to throw him (*kake* or execution); and allow you to finish the technique. This last aspect is normally considered as part of the second, but many judo players, in both *randori* and contest, fail to finish techniques because they think that the throw is over once the opponent has been catapulted into the air and is heading for the mat. In the days when everyone was taught to breakfall and safety was felt to be more important than winning and losing, this was usually the case. But these days most competition players devote a certain amount of training time in *randori* to gymnastic spin-outs and twists to avoid landing with their backs on the mat, even if it is only when someone actually attempts to throw them. A good grip in the first instance, and proper hand control right to the end of the technique, prevents them from doing this effectively. In addition, if ippon is not scored you will almost certainly be in a better position to immediately follow up with effective *newaze* if you have a good grip on your opponent rather than if you let go of him or her.

As most judo books cover the basic throw-

Figs 9–11 *The orthodox sleeve and lapel grip: ideal for classic forward throws such as this fine* tai-otoshi *by Karen Briggs on Lynn Poirier of Canada in the semi-final of the Commonwealth games. Note how the three times World Champion's undergrasp allows her to get right under her opponent's defence.*

Fig 10 *A fine pull from the left arm draws the Canadian fighter completely off balance over the stretched right leg which blocks any chance of escape.*

Fig 11 *Excellent finishing control is achieved by driving the right forearm under her armpit and employing an aggressive downwards pulling action with the hands. Combined with the rotation from the hips and the drive from the legs, Miss Poirier has no chance of avoiding the ippon – a near perfect throw.*

ing opportunities with both fighters in a square stance holding right-handed, the majority of the techniques demonstrated in this book will show opposing grips – right-handed against left. The positions covered can obviously be reversed so that the left-handed player can also see the appropriateness of the application of the various grips to different situations.

A fundamental characteristic which most effective throwing techniques exhibit is gripping skills which allow the thrower to get past the defender's arms. This is basic to any throw, whether the initial grip be undergrasp, overgrasp or even a leg grab. The arms are the first line of defence. Techniques which go under the arms require great skill, dexterity and speed; the amount of body contact they offer is relatively slight and its duration always momentary. Such throws need only rarely be forced. Techniques which go over the arms tend to require more strength in the thrower's upper body and often depend on effective body contact and head control for their success. Such techniques can be forced when they meet resistance and tend to be preferred by physically strong players who are perhaps less supple.

For the purpose of studying grips, the following categories can be used to group together and also distinguish certain interchangeable types of throw which proceed from the basic sleeve lapel or sleeve collar grip.

Forward throws involving getting underneath the opponent's arms, e.g. *tai-otoshi, seoi-nage, tomoe-nage.*
Forward throws relying upon head control, e.g. *uchimata, harai-goshi.*
Rear throws involving head control, e.g. *osoto-gari* and *kouchi-gari..*
Rear throws involving coming inside the opponent's arms, e.g. *ouchi-gari* and *kouchi-gari.*
Sideways or circling throws involving sweep-

Fig 12 Pesniak of the Soviet Union scores ippon with uchimata *on Kollanen of Finland with an orthodox left-hand undergrasp. Note the left elbow well tucked into the opponent's side chest and controlling the head, and the right hand pulling the left sleeve right around.*

ing the opponent's feet away, e.g. *yoko tomoe-nage* (sideways) and *sasae tsuri-komi-ashi* (circling).
Throws where the attacker moves to the side of the arms, e.g. *osoto-gari* and *kosoto-gari*.

I have grouped the throws in this way to illustrate the different operations that the basic grip allows and to clarify the sometimes subtle differences in the way that the grip functions in each type of technique.

The importance of the grip

An effective grip is the first step in the development of judo skills and in the attainment of contest excellence. In the early days of judo in this country it was considered against the spirit of judo to break your training partner's grip. Players allowed one another their preferred hold by mutual consent and then began to move around the mat looking for an opportunity to exploit any weakness or lack of concentration.

Times have changed. Judo is a dynamic, modern combat sport and the first stage of that combat is coming to grips with the opponent. Grip fighting requires good reflexes and hand speed, and considerable strength in the shoulders and forearms. In contest the battle for grips normally determines the eventual outcome of the match. If you want to do your techniques, you have to be able to get your grip. In *randori* a certain amount of grip fighting is essential, but this should not take over training at the expense of practising throwing skills. *Randori* has to involve a certain amount of give and take, otherwise it can become a very negative exercise.

Types of grip

The types of grip that can be seen in modern-day judo are many and varied, but the mainstays of most fighter's repertoires remain the orthodox sleeve and lapel grips.

The essential skills of judo are developed from these grips and they allow the wide range of classical techniques which make judo such an interesting and attractive sport. These are the safest and easiest grips from which to begin learning judo techniques, and they are normally the first basic grips that the beginner is taught. Unfortunately, they are often the only grips to be taught systematically.

Even within the group of orthodox grips there is an immense variety. Frequently, an 'orthodox' grip will combine with an extreme right or left stance or an extreme defensive *jigotai*, vastly different from the upright, natural posture taught to beginners.

People often mistakenly assume that because something is taught at beginner level

19

it will not then be effective at the level of a World Championship or the Olympic games. This is a misconception: anything taught at beginner level should be taught precisely *because* it can work however difficult the competition. Judo is a supremely rational sport, often described as physical chess, and the key to effectiveness is frequently the grip. Different grips are more or less appropriate against different types of fighter. Everyone has contrasting strengths and weaknesses.

Even Yamashita confessed that he could be thrown and occasionally was, in *randori*, when he allowed his training partners to get a collar grip and pull his head down. Contest, though, was a different story. His judo was built around his grip and everything else proceeded from it. In contest his left arm was as impassable as a steel bar; his right-hand grip on his opponents' sleeves was unbreakable. In his judo the complexities of gripping skill made the ippon throw appear inevitable.

Figs 14–16 *In this sequence of Karen Briggs doing* tomoe-nage *in a demonstration and in contest, good sleeve control is evident. Her basic sleeve and lapel grip for* tai-otoshi, ouchi-gari *or* yoko-tomoe-nage *is the same, so that the throw is very difficult to predict.*

Fig 15 *The basic grip allows the attacker to get well underneath her opponent with* tomoe-nage, *opening up her posture by pulling up and out with the hands.*

Fig 13 *An excellent example of left* harai-goshi *using the traditional sleeve and lapel grip by Auffray of France on Hansen of Denmark at the 1975 World Championship middleweight category – the epitome of stylish judo.*

Fig 16 *People who are good at the kind of handstand defence shown here by Ann Marie Mulholland might be more effectively thrown by the end-of-sleeve grip preventing them from walking on their hands.*

Yamashita exemplified the effectiveness of a basic left-handed grip through possessing the entirely enviable ability always to impose his grip and so dominate his opponents. His grip fighting was really quite simple. Normally he would come forward with arms open and allow his opponent to grip as they pleased, then he would simply take hold of their right lapel with his left hand. Once he had this grip he retained it. Often people sensed the danger immediately and would pull their left sleeve free. But they then had a problem because he was quite squat and thus difficult to attack with, for instance, *ippon seoi-nage*, as well as very effective at *shime-waza*. Also, as Yamashita wanted to get on with the business, so he would openly offer his right sleeve for his opponent to take. If the opponent did not take it, and did not attack either, he would eventually be penalised for passivity. As soon as the opponent gripped Yamashita's right sleeve he would take their left. Once the left sleeve was gripped he could attack. This simple routine was the key to his effectiveness.

Angelo Parisi of France was another top fighter who never seemed to grip fight, rather allowing his opponent to take his hold first. Only then would he take his own grip. The distinguished Japanese teacher Kisaburo Watanabe, talking about Parisi's judo and his incredibly relaxed but powerful ability to switch from left to right, called it 'Dream Judo'. With his double lapel grip, Parisi could throw with *seoi-otoshi*, *oguruma*, *osoto-gari*, *hiza-guruma* and *tai-otoshi*, at the very highest level.

Sleeve and lapel grip

The basic classical grip involves holding the sleeve and the lapel. I have always fought from a basic right-handed stance and grip, so I will describe the following techniques as proceeding from this grip.

To perform a right-handed throw such as *tai-otoshi*, the left hand grips the opponent's right sleeve and the right hand holds at about mid-

Fig 17 A superb attack by Angelo Parisi against the much taller Clemens Jehle of Switzerland. Note how Parisi favours the double lapel grip and how he tucks his right elbow inside Jehle's jacket, tightening the grip and increasing the effectiveness of the pull.

lapel. This is the ideal grip to bring off a *tai-otoshi*, especially when practising with someone of the same height or taller, but there are advantages and disadvantages to every grip.

With an orthodox sleeve and lapel grip there are only a limited number of throws that can be done to the opposite side. It would, for example, be extremely difficult and probably not very effective to attempt left *harai-goshi* from such a right-handed grip. The leverage would be all wrong and you would get tangled up. Left *seoi-nage*, *hiza-guruma* to either side and a variety of *ashi-waza* are the most probable and practical combinations and alternatives when using this grip.

High collar grip

The taller fighter often chooses to grip his opponent's collar at the neck, shifting the

21

Figs 19–21 Dave Starbrook throws Jan Bosman of Holland for ippon with a superb double lapel grip 'wrong leg' tai-otoshi. The Dutchman completely avoids Starbrook's outstretched left leg with his left foot, but is pinned to the Englishman's side by the extremely powerful pulling action of the hands.

Fig 18 Another harai-goshi, this time right-handed and from a double lapel grip by Veritchev of the Soviet Union on Zaprianov of Bulgaria in the heavyweight category at the 1986 European Championships.

right hand higher in order to control his opponent's head. This grip allows beginners with a feeling for hip throws to get in for their techniques and, provided they learn correct control of the opponent's head, it can be very effective. The high collar grip allows very good front and back combinations, the *harai-goshi* into *kosoto-gari* 'Twitch' being the most obvious. Experts in this sort of technique throw people by exploiting their conditioned defensive reflexes, and when successful these throws are spectacular.

Fig 20 Although Bosman manages to get his left foot well advanced to step around the throw in the conventional form of evasion, as Starbrook drives with the legs and rotates his shoulders he has to lift his right foot and is driven over his left supporting foot.

Fig 21 The direction of the application of force is very unusual in this example; note how the left hand forces the Dutchman's head down as the right pulls him around. The superb upper body control is apparent from the tension visible in Bosman's jacket. Superb technique allows Starbrook's formidable strength to be translated into an unstoppable throw. The downward pulling action of the hands is extremely fast and aggressive.

Double lapel grip

The double lapel grip is taught as a method of throwing both sides with the same technique, but care has to be taken that beginners do not injure themselves by putting out their arms as they are thrown.

Waist grip

People who are very strong in the arms sometimes like to pass their right arm under

Fig 22 *Katsuki, the 1979 Japanese World Champion at under 71kg, throws Landart of France for ippon in the final of the Paris Multi-nations. The Japanese has turned in and under Landart with left seoi-nage, against his strong defensive right arm. The rotational force of the body turning folds the arm under, trapping it against Katsuki's body. Good sleeve control with the left hand makes any kind of defence by putting out the arms impossible.*

the opponent's left arm and round his back, as in a basic *ogoshi*.

Basic Japanese styles

When the Japanese discuss grips they always relate them to stance and posture. They describe gripping situations in one of two ways. When a right-handed fighter meets another right-handed fighter they call it *ai-yotsu*, which means that both fighters are taking the same grip, either both right or both left. If the fighters are not symmetrical, with one left-handed and the other right-handed, this is called *kenka-yotsu*, opposite or opposing grips. All top Japanese fighters train to be able to deal effectively with these two basic situations so that they can handle both right- and left-handed fighters. Most Japanese take sleeve and lapel grips and rarely switch from gripping left to right, although they routinely do combinations like right *uchimata* and left *seoi-nage* which do not involve changing.

Another classical switch of the direction of attack common with the classical grip is the use of *sode-tsuri-komi-goshi*. A predominantly right-handed player who can do left *sode-tsuri-komi-goshi* has a major weapon at his

disposal. The beauty of the technique again is that no change of grip is necessary, so it is difficult to anticipate. Often the player will feint a right-handed attack first, then switch left, driving the arm across the opponent's face or even straight up in the air. Keith Remfry pulled off one of the major surprises of the 1971 World Judo Championships when he threw the reigning All-Japan Champion Iwata with this technique on the way to a bronze medal in the heavyweight category.

Solutions to opposing grips

Many of the less orthodox jacket grips are the result of trying to find a way to deal with a *kenka-yotsu* situation. In my case this was when I found myself facing a left-hander. Different grips are more or less suitable against different types of left-handed opponent: gripping the right sleeve with the left hand and around the back of the upper arm with the right was often effective against left-handed fighters who basically stood square. Such fighters often fell for a *sasae* or *hiza-*

Fig 23 *Right versus left (Janos Gyani versus Peter Seisenbacher). The left-handed fighter usually has a very strong defence because of his hip position – a simple turn of the hips easily allows him to block most right-handed forward throws. Cross gripping is a useful ploy for the right hander for pulling the upper body and hips around into an attackable position.*

23

Fig 24 *A good example of an attack with* eri-seoi-otoshi *as I come in low on Lepaubin of France in a European team contest. Even though my right knee is on the floor it is important to be able to use the leg to drive up and complete the throw.*

guruma, against their left legs after an initial feint with right *osoto* or *uchimata*.

Another style of fighter who preferred an extreme left stance could not be fought effectively from this grip because I could never reach for the opponent's right sleeve with my left hand without putting myself in danger. In such cases a cross grip from an extreme right stance, using the right hand to hold his right lapel, proved more effective. The right arm blocked most of the opponent's techniques and forced him to reach for my left sleeve, which allowed me to grip his right sleeve and attack in a flash with *yama-arashi*, or *eri-seoi-*

Fig 25 *Nobutoshi Hikage of Japan, twice World Champion, attacking the strong defensive arm of his opponent, Herrer of Cuba, to break the cross grip more than as an all-out attempt to throw. It is especially effective because there is also an armlock threat.*

otoshi as some people prefer to describe it. This cross grip was particularly good for pulling the extreme left-hander's hips around into a position where he could be effectively attacked.

Multi-direction seoi-nage

A throw frequently seen in contest which allows a rapid stance change is *seoi-nage*, done with both hands gripping one lapel. This is often learned as the throw to the other side by many fighters, as it allows them to switch sides without altering their basic lapel grip whether they are predominantly right- or left-handed. Initially, the thrower may have his left hand on his opponent's right lapel and attack left, for example with *uchimata*, then he may release his sleeve grip with his right hand and switch to the right, catching the right lapel with his right hand near his left hand. The same technique can work if introduced suddenly by either player when both players have one hand on and are standing square, or are in opposite stances fighting for sleeve control with their free hands. Paul Radburn of Great Britain was very effective with this technique against some very big heavyweights, pulling them around in a circle to get them moving and confuse them before launching himself underneath and driving them over the top.

Using the jacket skirt

The current crop of French fighters have increasingly begun to use the skirt of the jacket to bring off throws when the opponent's sleeve is unavailable. This sort of technique has evolved as a consequence of the increasing prevalence of tailored kits which make getting an effective grip more difficult. The decision by the International Judo Federation taken in 1990 to ban tailored kits forced fighters to wear more easily gripped jackets in the hope that there will be a decrease in negative judo.

Double sleeve grip

In the days when there were no weight categories in judo, the double sleeve grip was popular and orthodox among small men, especially when fighting bigger, heavier opponents. It remains effective even in weight category judo, but it is perhaps seen less often in practice. When used effectively the results can be really quite spectacular and, since the opponent at best has only one hand on a sleeve or lapel himself and both his shoulders are controlled, it is extremely difficult for him to avoid ippon once the technique begins.

Fig 27

Figs 26–30   The double sleeve grip used effectively by European Champion Amiran Toticachvilli, who threw Patrick Roux of France in the final of the European Championships in 1988. Roux had just taken hold with his left hand in the opening seconds when Toticachvilli grabbed the ends of his sleeves and spun in for the throw. The action of the throw is more like seoi-nage than the traditional sode-tsuri-komi-goshi at this stage.

Fig 27   Roux, despite his superior height and long arms is unable to get a hand out to block the throw which is the normal ploy when attacked by seoi-nage type techniques.

Fig 28

Fig 28   Because the long-legged Frenchman is almost able to block the throw by stepping over, Toticachvilli springs him over by driving with his right leg and diving his head towards the mat, swinging up the left leg uchimata-style to accentuate this.

Fig 29   Roux just manages to prevent the ippon by landing on his head.

Fig 30   He rolls on to his shoulders though which earns the Russian waza-ari and puts him in a perfect position to hold the Frenchman for a further twenty-five seconds with kami-shiho-gatame to win the contest.

Fig 29

Fig 26

Fig 30

Where and how to grip the judogi (Figs 32–38)

Fig 31 The mid-sleeve grip showing basic hand position for any right-handed sleeve lapel throw.

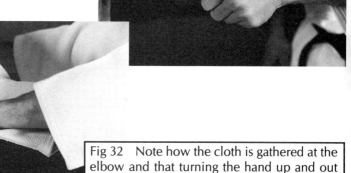

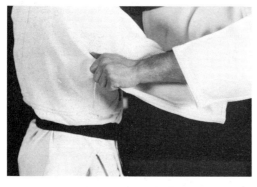

Fig 32 Note how the cloth is gathered at the elbow and that turning the hand up and out puts tension in the jacket to give a tight, controlling effect on the arm and in turn on the shoulder.

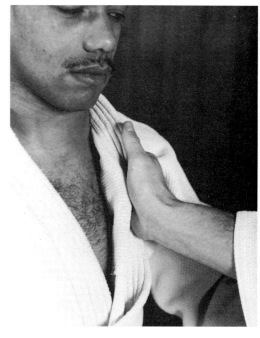

Fig 33 A slightly higher than normal grip on the arm can provide extra control if an opponent is wearing a baggy or loose kit.

Fig 34 The basic hand position for the right hand in a right-handed technique. The four fingers grip the opponent's jacket mid-lapel. Note that the thumb remains open to avoid the stiffening of the wrists that tends to accompany tight gripping with the thumb.

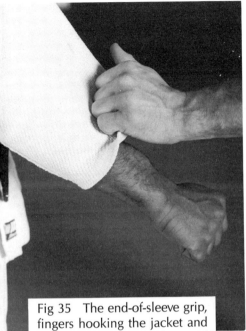

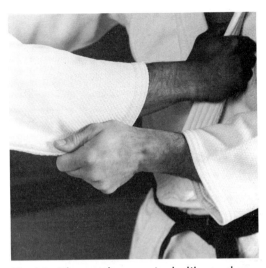

Fig 36   Those who genuinely like to throw from an end-of-sleeve grip are still permitted to do so as long as they grip underneath, not on top of the sleeve.

Fig 35   The end-of-sleeve grip, fingers hooking the jacket and pushing the opponent's arm down. Although exceptionally strong, this grip is now illegal as it is felt to be overly defensive and once imposed prevents the opponent from doing positive, attacking judo.

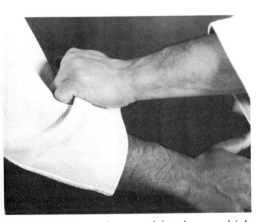

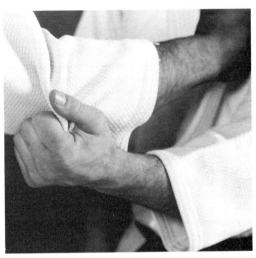

Fig 37   A grip on the top of the sleeve, which is very useful for gripping defensively and is legal; the middle of the sleeve rather than the end has to be gripped.

Fig 38   The sleeve grip does not necessarily always pull, sometimes it is used for pushing when a change of direction is in order. This undergrasp can be useful for controlling the elbow and makes for a powerful lifting action in techniques like *hiza-guruma* and *sasae-tsuri-komi-ashi*.

27

Gripping to develop pulling power (Fig 39a and b)

A common method of developing pulling power, particularly the *hikite* or left-hand pull from the orthodox grip which is a basic technique for getting past stiff, resisting arms.

Fig 39a Starting position for practising *uchikomi* intended to develop pulling power.

Fig 39b Pulling up and out allows entry for techniques such as *uchimata* and *harai-goshi*. This *uchikomi* drill exaggerates the up and out action of the pull for maximum effectiveness.

Directions of pull (Fig 40a–c)

The effectiveness of any technique is determined not just by getting a usable grip but by ensuring that the grip is used to apply the pull in the most appropriate direction. The pull is not the same for all forward throws; *tai-otoshi* is quite different in feeling to *harai-goshi* and rear throws are even more different. One very important ability is that of changing the direction of an attack – making a push into a pull and vice versa.

Fig 40a In this simple example I have an orthodox right-handed grip as does uke.

Fig 40b I step back and draw my opponent off balance over his right leg, because he does not want to step and follow.

Synchronising the hands and the feet (Fig 41a and b)

It is important to practise synchronising your footwork with your partner or opponent.

Fig 41a Practise *tsugi-ashi* (following footwork). As you step back draw him forwards, as he steps back you follow.

Fig 40c I can thus easily drop into position for *tai-otoshi*. The left hand pulls continuously, the right turns from a pull into a push and the feeling is almost of punching him into the ground on completion. If my opponent does step then I can attempt *kouchi-gari* as he puts his foot down and sweep away his right foot – the direction of pull in this case is down and out with the left hand as the right pushes back and down.

Fig 41b All the time look for the timing to do an appropriate technique, concentrate on getting hands and feet working together.

Attacking pairs of techniques from less orthodox grips

Different grips facilitate different techniques but, because the less orthodox grips tend to telegraph the thrower's intentions more than the classic sleeve and lapel grip, it is important to have at the very least pairs of techniques allowing directional switches that exploit the defender's reactions.

Right arm around the shoulder grip (Fig 42)

Fig 42 The right arm around the shoulder grip is a very useful technique against fighters who like to grip left-handed and defend by

stiffening the left arm. It is a powerful grip allowing you to use the power of the back and arm to bend your opponent's resisting arm trapping it against the side of your chest as you attack. This grip allows the thrower to switch sides very effectively.

Uchimata and sasae-tsuri-komi-ashi (Fig 43a–g)

A particularly useful pair of throws that work well in combination are *uchimata* and *sasae-tsuri-komi-ashi* (or *hiza-guruma* depending on the relative lengths of arms and legs).

Fig 43a Uke is holding with his left hand. I stand extreme right and grip around his left shoulder with my right hand and hold mid-sleeve undergrasp with the left.

Fig 43b I turn in for *uchimata* by stepping across in front of uke with my right foot and turning my hips anticlockwise and then transfer my weight on to my left foot which I place just inside his left foot.

Fig 43c From this cocked position it is easy to drive my hips back between my opponent's legs and use the springing action of my legs to drive him into the air.

Fig 43d The over-the-shoulder grip ensures good control for finishing the technique as well as good contact throughout the attack between my side chest and his. Normally in a *randori* situation your partner reacts to having been thrown with *uchimata* from this grip by stiffening up and trying to push you off the next time you attack.

Fig 43e I can feel my opponent resisting the threat of my *uchimata*.

Fig 43f I feint the *uchimata* with a quick tug of the hands and quickly change direction, making a large step across in front of him to my left on my left foot.

Fig 43g As soon as my left foot touches the mat I spin my head to my right, looking over my right shoulder and turning his upper body to my right as I rotate. Pulling down and around with the right hand and pushing up with the left on his right arm, I block his ankle or knee to whirl him over my outstretched leg.

Cross lapel grip and yama-arashi (Fig 44a–d)

Cross lapel grip with the right hand lends itself particularly well to fighting strong left-handers who have an extreme left stance. The grip allows you to pull your opponent around until his hips are square and less difficult to attack.

Fig 44a   I have my cross grip and use it defensively to hold off my opponent in order to set him up for *yama-arashi*.

Fig 44b   I keep my left sleeve well away from him so he is forced to step forwards on his right foot if he is to reach for it.

Fig 44c   Once he steps into this square on position I quickly take a grip on his right sleeve with my left hand.

Fig 44d   I can now attack effectively with a good chance of success – in a flash I turn underneath him with *yama-arashi*.

Right cross grip and left seoi-nage (Fig 45a–d)

A linked attack from the cross grip which is yet another alternative to either of the two previous techniques. With any right cross grip attack is to switch and do left *ippon-seoi-nage*. This can come as a real surprise to many left-handed fighters.

Fig 45a My opponent is holding with his left hand and I am gripping his right lapel with a right-hand cross grip. It is very difficult for him to get an effective grip with his right hand if he maintains this left stance.

Fig 45b As my opponent begins to step forwards on his right foot in an attempt to grip with his right hand, I relax my stiff right arm. I then step in on my left foot and begin to pull up with my right hand in a classic *hikite* action for left *seoi-nage*.

Fig 45c Despite having the 'wrong' grip I can turn in very effectively for *ippon-seoi-nage*, taking my opponent completely by surprise.

Fig 45d As you have less control of your opponent's shoulder with this grip than with a more orthodox one, it is important to control his or her left arm with your left hand – if not, he or she may well react to your attack later in the throw by doing a handstand. Gathering up the arm overcomes this type of defence.

Fig 46 Another classic tai-otoshi *by champion Paul Sheals on Fitzroy Davis in the final of the Commonwealth games which earned him a waza-ari and the title of Commonwealth Champion. Note the control transmitted through the tension in Davis's jacket. Only Davis's impressive agility prevented ippon being scored.*

The shrug (Figs 47–49)

An important function of the right hand in many right-handed throwing techniques is to get past the defender's left arm. This is especially true if he is mainly left-handed.

Fig 47 Gripping with the thumb closed gives a strong hold, but primarily a defensive one since it makes the wrists stiff and makes it more difficult to turn in for techniques.

Fig 48 Gripping with the fingers and keeping the thumb open allows more dexterity in the wrists and forearms and in turn makes it easier to move the shoulders and open up your opponent for an attack.

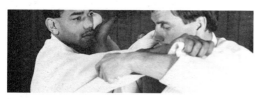

Fig 49 By turning the hand until it is almost palm up and then bending the elbow, it is possible to slip the right shoulder inside his defensive left hand. This allows the thrower to attack with the technique he prefers. *Seoi-otoshi*, or *tai-otoshi* are personal favourites. It is sometimes known as the 'shrug' because of the feeling of shrugging off an opponent's grip.

Head control

Head control can be achieved by a variety of grips but the orthodox sleeve and lapel grip is surprisingly versatile and can be used for both forward and backward techniques. Throws like *harai-goshi* and *uchimata* sometimes rely on good head control to be effective. Failing to control an opponent's head when you hold high and make a one-legged forward throw leaves you very vulnerable to being picked up with a counter-throw.

Fig 50 The inimitable Michel Nowak of France, in an aggressive mood, has such good head control that the East German Lehmann's jacket is like a rope around his head. Nowak can attack with a lateral osoto-gari with little fear of being picked up and can change into a harai-goshi makikomi action if his opponent overdefends the threat to the rear. The main weakness of the grip is that both of the opponent's arms are free to grab the leg and hips for a possible counter. Either player might be thrown for ippon when such an attack is attempted, but Nowak has the advantage because of his grip, which allows him to drive his body-weight down on to his attacking leg.

Head control in forward throws (Fig 51a and b)

This sequence shows the importance of head control when fighting right-handed against a strong right-hander. The deep collar grip can be safely held because the extreme right stance and my sleeve control of my opponent's right hand make it impossible for him to try *seoi-nage* against the right arm.

Fig 51a By stepping away from my opponent diagonally and allowing my arms to straighten I can use my moving body-weight to draw him behind me, setting him up for an attack with *uchimata*. I can then swing in against him, pulling him on to the throw. The pull at this point is forwards and up.

Fig 51b As my leg sweeps up and I bend my body forwards at the waist my hands pull my opponent down and around, driving his head towards the mat. I retain control of my opponent right to the end, coming down on top of him to ensure that he does not twist out.

The slip (Fig 52a and b)

This sequence shows right *uchimata* against a left-handed fighter.

Fig 52a Initially I have an orthodox sleeve and lapel grip, but I have made sure to loosen my opponent's jacket. He is not expecting *uchimata* because the grip does not give any indication of the intended attack.

Fig 52b As I turn in, I simultaneously slip the lapel upwards so the back of my wrist goes around his neck. As I continue to turn, my right-hand grip pushes his head forwards and down, unbalancing him to his front right. The element of surprise afforded by slipping my grip around the back of his neck makes it relatively easy to lift him with *uchimata*.

Head control in rear attacks (Fig 53a–c)

Fig 53a   A fairly high grip on the lapel allows me to attack with *osoto-gari*, without making it obvious that this is my intention.

Fig 53b   I slip the lapel over my opponent's shoulder and drive my forearm into the side of his face.

Fig 53c   This use of the forearm allows me to tip his head backwards by lifting the right elbow up as I simultaneously strike with my reaping leg. By pulling his right arm into my body and down and tipping his head backwards, his balance is broken completely and an ippon score is probable. If a smaller score were awarded the head control allows me to go into *kesa-gatame* immediately.

Failure to control the head (Fig 54a and b)

Fig 54a   Shows the danger of failing to control the head and of pulling down instead of up with the left hand in a *harai-goshi* attack. attack right against right (*ai-yotsu*).

Because of poor *hikite* (pull), my opponent is able to keep a straight back and simply has to bend the knees and lift to counter with *ura-nage*.

Fig 54b   Once in this position the chances of conceding a score are great.

Kenkya-yotsu (opposing grips)

Kouchi-gari (Fig 55a–c)

This is a common situation in judo when a right-handed player finds himself up against a left-hander. Depending upon the styles of the two fighters, more or less extreme stances may be adopted. When a left-handed fighter chooses to defend, it is more difficult for the right-handed fighter to attack effectively with a traditional sleeve and lapel grip. The first step is often to get the undergrasp with the right hand. Together with the sleeve grip this makes it possible to open an opponent up for attack.

Fig 55b The pulling action of the arms is down and out as his balance is broken.

Fig 55a Starting from a position slightly to the left of my opponent, I find *kouchi-gari* is particularly useful for opening up a left-handed defence. By pulling the arms apart and coming in diagonally to reap the right leg, the left-handed fighter's defence is nullified.

Fig 55c As well as keeping up a continuous pull with both hands it is important to drive your weight into the technique to throw him flat on his back to score ippon. If you start the technique from too far out you may find that you lack the necessary extension to get him flat on his back. If you do only score a knock-down be sure to follow up straight away with *newaza*.

Tai-otoshi (Fig 56a–d)

Fig 56a Another possible solution to a *kenka-yotsu* situation, this time using *tai-otoshi*. Starting once again with the end-of-sleeve grip, I ensure that I have the undergrasp with both the left and right hands. This time I position myself slightly to the right of my opponent and push against him to give the impression of some kind of rear threat, for instance *osoto-gari*.

Fig 56b When I feel either resistance or uncertainty, I make my attack. I pull up and out with the left arm, turning the little finger edge up and out, and draw with the right, turning my hand in the direction of the throw. simultaneously pivot on my right foot so that can throw my left foot behind me, placing just outside my opponent's left foot.

Ouchi-gari (Fig 57a–c)

Fig 57a Right *ouchi-gari* is effective against left-handed fighters in a *kenka-yotsu* situation. It is important, however, that the grip from which you attack with *ouchi* should be the same as the grip that you use for your major forwards techniques, such as *tai-otoshi* and *uchimata*, which combine particularly well because of the strong defensive reaction they elicit.

ig 56c As my opponent is pulled off
alance I off-load the weight from my left leg
nd stab my right leg across in front of him,
iming to catch him just below the knee with
ne back of my bent leg.

Fig 56d To make the throw, I snap the leg
straight, adding this spring to the pull of the left
hand and drive him over it, turning him on to
his back with the combined action of the left
arm pulling, the right hand pushing and the
shoulders turning. The feeling on completion of
the throw is of punching the right hand into the
mat as the left hand pulls towards the ceiling.

Fig 57b Starting roughly square on to my
opponent I step across with my right foot and
begin to pivot, swinging the left foot around
behind me. At this point I could do *tai-otoshi*,
osoto-gari or *uchimata*.

Fig 57c Instead, since I feel him pulling back
to his left rear, I switch into *ouchi-gari* and clip
his left leg with my right, pulling down with
my hands so that his weight is pinned over the
attacked leg.

Action of the right hand in ouchi-gari (Fig 58a–c)

Fig 58a The right hand is often a problem in doing *ouchi-gari*. Many fighters like to drive it straight over their opponent's shoulder just above the collar bone to get more weight on to the leg being attacked. Others like to loop the jacket over the shoulder to reduce the opponent's chances of twisting off the technique. Some like to just hang.

> Note one danger with using *ouchi-gari* against a strong left-handed player, though, is the possibility his grip affords him of doing a *kosoto-gari* counter-throw. His left-hand grip gives him good control of the right side of my body. If he pulls down strongly he can counter spectacularly by hooking my leg. This is called *ouchi-gaeshi* because it occurs so often in *randori* and contest.

(a)

Preventing ouchi-gaeshi (Fig 59a–c)

Fig 59a By releasing the right hand and driving it down over the defender's left arm, thereby pinning his shoulder and all his weight over the attacked leg, the danger from the left arm is nullified.

Fig 59b The free right hand can then slide down and catch the defender's hip as he tries to step back off the technique.

The right hand can even drop to grip his leg if necessary, preventing any possibility of stepping off the technique.

Fig 59c If he attempts to counter with *ouchi-gaeshi* in this position he will certainly be thrown as both his left arm and left leg are effectively pinned.

Optional head control in ouchi-gari (Fig 60)

Fig 60 The action of the right hand is not limited to pulling or pushing on the lapel where it grips. It can be particularly useful for controlling the opponent's head by pushing up under the chin in order to get the head going backwards in techniques like *osoto-gari* and *kouchi-gari*. Many smaller fighters use these techniques to great effect against bigger opponents.

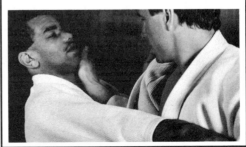

Head control in kenkya-yotsu (Fig 61)

Fig 61 Releasing the lapel and gripping around the head is another useful method of getting head control for forward throws such as *harai-goshi* and *koshi-guruma*. It must, however, be used to attack with immediately, as the contact it offers the person being attacked is very good for dustbin techniques like *uranage* if the throw does not come off.

Deep collar grip in kenkya-yotsu (Fig 62)

Fig 62 Gripping the collar at the back of the opponent's neck with the thumb in is a good alternative to wrapping the whole arm around him. The thumb edge of the hand gives very good head control for forward throws.

Ashi-waza with the around-the-shoulder grip (Fig 63a–b)

Fig 63a Another technique which the around-the-shoulder grip can enhance is *okuri-ashi-barai*.

Fig 63b Because the left-handed fighter's left arm is pulled in and trapped in the bent position, he has no opportunity to put an arm out to save himself from being thrown once his feet are swept away. From the thrower's point of view the hand action of the throw is like turning a steering wheel, the right hand pulling down as the left drives upwards.

Pulling the right side of the body around (Fig 64a–e)

Fig 64a Another form of one-armed shoulder throw involves pinning the opponent in a bent posture by grabbing his right sleeve with my left hand, then gripping the back of his right sleeve with my right hand either behind his shoulder or if possible at the back of the armpit.

Fig 64b This is a very strong grip which pins all his weight on one side of his body. It is possible for me to throw with an *osoto-gari* action or, as in this case, with *seoi-nage* – I simply pull myself in on the arm.

Fig 64c Having stepped forwards on my right foot I turn my hips and attack with *seoi-nage*.

Fig 64d If my opponent attempts to jump around the technique I drop my right arm to facilitate the turning of my opponent's hips.

Fig 64e This dropping of the arm helps me to unload him off my shoulder and accelerates the turning of his hips and the speed of his fall.

Ai-yotsu (same grips)
Osoto-gari, diagonal entry (Fig 65a–c)

This sequence shows a diagonal entry for *osoto-gari* in order to get past an opponent's stiff, resisting arms.

Fig 65a   This is an *ai-yotsu* situation as both fighters are holding right-handed. Note that the left hand initially pulls up and out to open up his defence as I attack.

Fig 65b   I take a big step across to my opponent's right with my left foot, bypassing the stiff arm resistance, rather than confronting it. From this position it is easy to swing my right leg through and behind my opponent's right leg.

Fig 65c   At the point of actually reaping away the leg, my left hand pulls down as my right hand begins to drive his head back and down in coordination with his reaping right leg.

Kouchi-gari, splitting the arms (Fig 66)

Fig 66   An alternative to going past the arms is to push them down and out by making a direct attack with *kouchi-gari*.

Tomoe-nage, getting under strong arms (Fig 67a–d)

Fig 67a   A right-handed grip does not always mean that you have to attack with a traditional right-handed technique. In this *yoko-tomoe-nage* I begin in a crouching posture, holding right-handed.

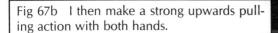

Fig 67b   I then make a strong upwards pulling action with both hands.

Fig 67c   Having made the initial pull, I could step in on my left foot, plant my right foot in his stomach, sit down and throw with an orthodox *tomoe-nage*. Instead, however, I swing my left foot up into his stomach and drop to the side, aiming to place my head near his left foot.

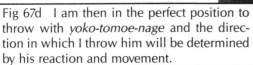

Fig 67d   I am then in the perfect position to throw with *yoko-tomoe-nage* and the direction in which I throw him will be determined by his reaction and movement.

Kouchi-gari, altering the angle of defence (Fig 68a–d)

Fig 68a In a right against right situation when your opponent adopts a very extreme stance, it is sometimes necessary to make big movements at speed to set him up for an appropriate technique. What you are doing in effect, by moving, is altering the angle of his defence, making it less extreme and at the same time less effective.

Fig 68b With *kouchi-gari* step to the side and forwards on your left foot and use your right hand to pull him around so that he is square on to you as he steps on to his left foot.

Fig 68c Immediately reap his right leg with *kouchi-gari*, remembering to pull down with the hands.

Fig 68d Remember to spring into the technique with your legs and aim to score ippon, not just a knock-down.

Tai-otoshi, altering the angle of attack (Fig 69a–d)

Fig 69a *Tai-otoshi* can work very well in an extreme right against right situation, but it requires the thrower to be very supple in the legs and hips.

Fig 69b Note how I make a very big circling step back around with the left foot as I pull up with the left hand. I then throw my body underneath my opponent by reaching right across with the right foot.

Fig 69c I bend both legs as I drop into the ideal position for throwing my opponent over my leg.

Fig 69d The combination of a fast, aggressive hand action and bending forwards at the waist means that all my body-weight is put into throwing my opponent in an effort to un-balance him. The straightening right leg and continuous pull from the hands finish the technique.

Seoi-nage, adapting to a grip
(Fig 70a–e)

Fig 70a Attacking left-handed from a right-handed grip is always a good ploy and tends to surprise an opponent, whether he is holding left or right. In this sequence I do *seoi-nage* from a basic overgrasp lapel grip when my opponent is holding right-handed and gripping my right sleeve with his left hand.

Fig 70b I push his right arm away with my left hand and step in left foot first, pivoting and following with the right.

Fig 70c Against a left-hand grip on my right lapel, the angle of entry has to be different.

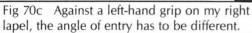

The slip (Fig 71a–c)

Fig 71a One popular defensive grip is the double lapel with a left arm undergrasp. A simple way to get past this defensive grip is to use the right elbow.

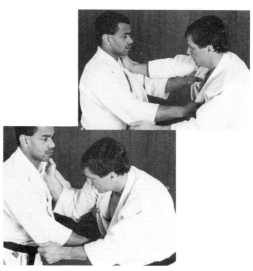

Fig 70d I attack again with left *seoi-nage*, but this time I pivot on the left foot and take the hips around in a big circle. The right foot lands between his feet first and the left follows it.

Fig 71b Slip the right elbow over the crook of his left arm and drive it down, bending his arm and your own at the same time. This simple manoeuvre puts you in the ideal position to attack with a variety of techniques, especially *uchimata* and *tai-otoshi*.

Fig 70e Note how the right forearm traps his left wrist against my chest. In the first attack I go mainly under the arm; in the second I go more to the side of it. The difference in grips makes the direction of the throw completely different in both cases.

Fig 71c Unless you attack immediately, he may sense the danger and disengage or try to reach around your back for some sort of left hip throw attack. If you let him grip with his left hand around your back before attacking him, you also risk being countered by some kind of pick up or *yoko-guruma*.

Sode-tsuri-komi-goshi: the switch (Fig 72a–c)

Fig 72a   The classic switch of direction from the traditional sleeve lapel grip is the *sode-tsuri-komi-goshi* on the other side. Here I grip right-handed, giving no hint that I intend to attack left.

Fig 72b   I turn in on the left, driving my opponent's right arm up in the air and pulling him across my hips with my right hand.

Fig 72c   Because my right hand was holding undergrasp his left arm is free, but providing I jack him up with my legs, rotate my hips and gain sufficient height, I should be able to throw him on his back even if he tries to defend by putting his arm out. An overgrasp would have allowed me to trap his arm against my body, but it might have given him a hint as to my intentions as I normally favour the undergrasp for right-handed attacks. These sort of things have to be practised on a variety of partners; experimentation will eventually indicate which grip is better in individual cases.

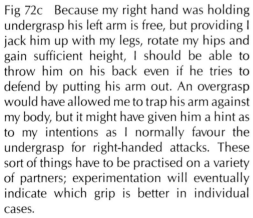

Kata-guruma (Fig 73a and b)

This is a technique which can be brought off from a variety of grips.

Fig 73a Holding the sleeve is a useful method since it affords excellent control of the opponent and prevents him from putting out the arm to attempt a handstand or cartwheel defence.

Fig 74 A classical grip for a classic throw. The sleeve leg grip employed by Japanese World Student Champion Takeshi Mizushima for his particular brand of kata-guruma. Note the right hand driving up as the left pulls down, creating a large circular motion.

Fig 73b The right arm hooks around the back of his thigh just above the knee, and the throwing action involves lifting with the right shoulder as you pull him down and over the back of your neck with your left hand.

51

Double lapel grip
(Figs 75 and 76)

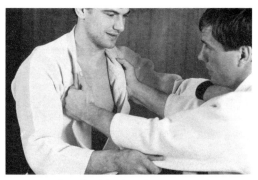

Fig 75 The double lapel grip is a favourite among players who are ambidextrous as it allows them to switch from left to right with ease. However, the grip shown here does not provide the thrower very good control of his opponent, since there is a tendency for the jacket to slip around his body.

Fig 77 An interesting attack by Andras Ozvar of Hungary on Alexander Van der Groeben of West Germany. Despite having a double lapel grip, Ozvar has controlled his opponent's arm by trapping it against his body with his forearm. Both hands are pulling well and the legs are driving effectively.

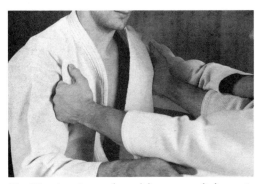

Fig 76 A grip preferred by many fighters is the mid-chest grip where, instead of gripping the lapel, the material between the chest and the armpits is gathered up. This gives very good control of the shoulders and makes it easier to control the opponent's upper body. Some techniques are more effective with one hand gripping mid-chest and the other gripping the lapel, depending upon the amount of cloth available and how tight the jacket is.

Fig 78 Vladimir Nevzerov versus Talaj. The Russian has attacked with a double lapel grip, turning his left hand as he rotates. Nevzerov lifts high with the leg before rotating to finish the throw, so that when the arm goes out to defend it gets pulled under (mid-chest grip).

Double lapel grip, high and low (Fig 79a and b)

The double lapel grip can be very useful for right-handed fighters when faced with a left-hander who keeps his sleeve from being gripped.

Fig 79a   By holding low with the left hand and high with the right a strong turning motion can be generated against awkward left-handers.

Fig 79b   This grip also allows the right arm to tuck under the opponent's armpit nicely. It can be a simple matter to attack with *tai-otoshi* once this sort of control is generated.

Double lapel grip for uchimata (Fig 80a–c)

The high and low double lapel grip is very useful against fighters who try to control the leading arm.

Fig 80a   As my opponent attempts to break my right-hand grip on his lapel I immediately catch the bottom of his right hand lapel with my left hand. This prevents him from breaking my grip and, as his grip is weak defensively, gives me a perfect opportunity to attack.

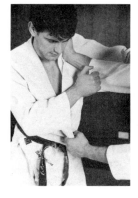

Fig 80b   I immediately turn in with *uchimata*.

Fig 80c   It is important to get sufficient height to ensure complete rotation as he does have his right hand free to prevent the throw.

Ogoshi grip (Fig 81a–c)

In the conventional *ogoshi* grip, the arm goes under the opponent's arm and around his waist, holding the belt at the back.

Fig 81a   This grip affords very good control of the opponent's lower body but it is important to emphasise the pull with the left hand or *hikite*.

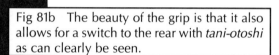

Fig 81b   The beauty of the grip is that it also allows for a switch to the rear with *tani-otoshi* as can clearly be seen.

Fig 81c   It is important to bend the knees in order to get well underneath him and to ensure his balance is effectively broken forwards by driving with the power of both legs as you pull with the arms.

Fig 82 Stephane Traineau of France exploits his long arms to good advantage with a grip on the belt around the arm allowing him to attack with tsuri-goshi.

Fig 83 From this grip he can evolve the technique into harai-goshi *or, as in this case,* uchimata, *to score a spectacular ippon.*

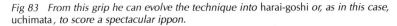

Grip and Attack:
Unorthodox Methods

In this chapter we shall be looking at the kinds of technique that proceed from grips other than the basic sleeve and lapel forms. The introduction of the more unorthodox gripping techniques which are increasingly common in modern international judo is a direct result of changes in fighting style from the classical Japanese judo form. When both men move around the mat with upright posture there is little chance or need to belt grab; both players can fight from a classical grip and attempt classical throws. When one or the other, or both, decides to adopt a deep-crouching defensive posture the situation changes dramatically and many of the classical techniques become increasingly awkward and difficult to apply.

When a person is bent over in a defensive posture at forty-five degrees to his opponent it requires considerable skill and dexterity to get underneath and throw. Taller players who like hip techniques tend to adopt a different approach, reaching over the shoulder to grip mid-back or even further to grab the belt. Once either grip is attained, they can generate tremendous lift and control for throws like *tsuri-goshi* or *harai-goshi*.

Some of the common unorthodox grips derive from Russian sombo wrestling. Others have evolved from changes in the rule structure of the sport: some grips which were once common have fallen into disuse because of the introduction of weight categories and restrictive changes in the rules.

Types of grip

Belt grips

There are numerous unusual jacket grips. A favourite among the Russians is gripping the sleeve or lapel, throwing the other arm over the shoulder and gripping the jacket at the back, which is particularly useful for doing hip throws like *harai-goshi* and *uchimata*. Fighters with good reach can even get the belt with this approach, which gives them considerably more purchase and control.

As well as providing extra purchase and control of the opponent's upper body in arm-over-the-back throws such as *tsuri-goshi*, a variety of *sutemi-waza* and takedowns have been evolved exploiting the belt. Many of these techniques are perennial favourites among Russian judo players with their strong tradition in sombo wrestling.

Except when performed supremely well these sort of techniques lack the aesthetic appeal of, for instance, an *uchimata* or a *tai-otoshi* done from an orthodox sleeve and lapel grip. On the other hand, they can be very effective: their very unexpectedness upsets many orthodox grippers and they are especially useful for leading into *newaza*. The Russian Shota Khabarelli frequently used to throw his opponents for ippon with *harai-goshi*, *uchimata*, *ouchi-gari* and a modified *uranage* which was almost an *uchimata* in reverse. The absolute master of this sort of belt gripping in order to take down an opponent into *newaza*, however, was Katsuhiko Kashiwazaki of Japan, 1981 under-65kg World Champion. He showed his great versatility by taking on the Russians at sombo and beating them at their own game, becoming a World Sombo Champion even before becoming World Judo Champion. His *tokui-waza* was *obi-tori-gaeshi* which he inevitably followed up with *tate-shiho-gatame* – a simple sequence which won him numerous contests.

Same-side grips

Kashiwazaki was not the only Japanese fighter to resort to the unorthodox. Shinobu Sekine before him, the World Middleweight Champion used to work from a same sleeve, same lapel grip, only doing major attacks like *ouchi-gari* and *kouchi-gari* and his own special *yoko-gake*.

The Japanese also introduced the two hands on one lapel *seoi-nage*, turning to the opposite side with fighters like Hidetoshi Nakanishi as defensive crouches and one-sided defensive gripping grew more extreme and it became increasingly difficult to catch people with the more well known techniques. This version is, however, much less likely to score ippon than the more conventional attack, but is good for folding up strong defensive arms through the powerful rotation action of the body and also has good potential for scoring with armlock follow-ups.

Leg grabs

Leg grabs are another branch of *tachi-waza* – they deserve special study as do the methods of taking grips appropriate to the particular variants applicable to certain opponents. Grabbing my opponent's right leg behind the knee with my left hand after forcing him to react backwards by threatening right *yama-arashi* was a particularly effective leg grab combination for me in a number of contests. Many coaches denigrate leg grabs as scrappy, belonging to the Rugby field and not the judo mat, but done well they are as attractive and effective as any other throw.

The 1980 Olympic Under-95kg Champion Robert Van de Walle has thrown dozens of people with his famous *morote-gari* in contest. Ben Spykers of Holland, 1988 Olympic bronze medallist at under 86kg, always does *morote-gari* when he is in a contest with ten seconds to go. He jumps up in the air, lifting both hands above head height, then drops

Fig 84   Chabil Biktachev throws Angelo Parisi with the typical Russian mid-back grip. Untidy, untraditional, but so very effective.

down into a crouch, grabbing his opponent behind the knees. When he gets both legs he does *morote-gari*, but if he manages to grab only one he tries *kosoto-gari* or *kouchi-gari*. Even though all his opponents on the international scene have seen him do this and expect it, amazingly it still works for him!

The leg grab is far from being the domain of the heavier weights, although as they are perhaps less agile bigger men may be easier to score on with it. Kashiwazaki, in the final of the Kano Cup, threw his great rival Sahara with an *ashi-tori ouchi-gari* that was so slick it was almost unbelievable. A good principle to remember is, having caught one leg always try to sweep the other as quickly as possible before your opponent gets a chance to adjust. With *ashi-tori ouchi-gari*, in particular, it is a good idea to make a half-turn to further break the opponent's balance and prevent him from twisting out of the technique.

Over-the-shoulder belt grabbing techniques

Tsuri-goshi: the Russian influence (Fig 85a–c)

The over-the-shoulder belt grip favoured by so many Soviet fighters can be very useful when the opponent adopts a defensive *jigotai* or crouch, but is difficult to obtain against an upright fighter.

Fig 85a Once you get this grip you must attack immediately and keep your opponent's head down throughout the attack.

Fig 85b If he manages to get his back straight, he can do a variety of pick-up counters.

Fig 85c The power of the throw comes from driving up with both legs after you have pinned his upper body to yours with an over-the-back grip.

Obi-tori-gaeshi (Fig 86a–d)

Obi-tori-gaeshi, is a take-down technique made famous by Katsuhiko Kashiwazaki of Japan.

Fig 86a I initiate this technique from an *ai-yotsu* situation.

Fig 86b A quick tug on the sleeve to get the opponent to bend over, and my right arm is instantly thrown over his right shoulder.

Fig 86c I grab the belt, thumb in. My left hand goes under his right arm, bending it, and I grab the back of his arm at the triceps. At this point I press down on his right shoulder with my right armpit to get him to push against me.

Fig 86d As he reacts, I place my left foot between his feet, sit down and flick him over with a *sumi-gaeshi* action with my right leg. Follow up into *newaza* with *tate-shiho* or *yoko-shiho-gatame*.

Obi-tori-gaeshi into harai-goshi combination (Fig 87a–d)

Many European fighters, once they manage to grip the belt over the top of the shoulder, like to attack with *osoto-gari* or *harai-goshi*, which work well in combination from this grip.

Fig 87a An important point to remember when going for this grip is that your opponent should already be in a bent over posture.

Fig 87b Attack as soon as the grip is obtained – some referees quickly penalise prolonged gripping of the belt. The defender, in reacting strongly to defend against an *osoto-gari* attack to the rear, often sets himself up to be thrown forwards.

Fig 87c Simply put the right foot on the floor and turn through ninety degrees, placing the left foot between your opponent's legs. Good contact between the armpit and shoulder and a long, continuous pull with the left hand are important to the success of the technique.

Fig 87d Finish the throw by sweeping your opponent's legs into the air and rotating from the waist with a *makikomi* action.

Attacking the leading arm

Many competitors like to fight extremely one-sided, offering as little of themselves to attack as possible, by gripping with one hand and keeping the other arm back. This has led to a number of techniques being developed for attacking the leading arm.

Tani-otoshi (Fig 88a–d)

Fig 88a This is a *kenkya-yotsu* situation in which *tani-otoshi* is particularly suitable. Initially I grip the opponent's left lapel with my right hand and can, if necessary, make *ashi-waza* attacks or even turn in for *uchimata* to confuse and upset him.

Fig 88b When the timing is right for the *tani-otoshi* I step behind him, dropping my right arm over his left arm and around his waist, catching him at the hip bone with my right hand.

Fig 88c The throw is made by pushing him to his right rear corner, pulling tightly with the left hand and bending the knees to sink the hips.

Fig 88d My opponent is thrown as I drive upwards with the power of both legs and pull with the arms to upend him.

Yoko-sutemi-waza (Fig 89a–d)

When attacking the leading arm it is not always necessary to allow your opponent to grip.

Fig 89a   For this *yoko-sutemi-waza* against a left-handed opponent, adopt a left stance, reach forward with your left hand and grab his left sleeve.

Fig 89b   Pull him slightly off balance forwards and step into him on your right foot. Simultaneously, throw your right arm over his shoulder and grab his jacket at the back of his belt.

Fig 89c   Keeping tight contact between your armpit and the top of his shoulder, step between his feet with your left foot, sit down and flick him over with a *sumi-gaeshi* action using the right leg.

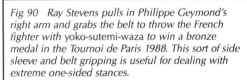

Fig 90   Ray Stevens pulls in Philippe Geymond's right arm and grabs the belt to throw the French fighter with yoko-sutemi-waza to win a bronze medal in the Tournoi de Paris 1988. This sort of side sleeve and belt gripping is useful for dealing with extreme one-sided stances.

Fig 89d   Turn your head to the right as you throw and be ready to follow up with *newaza*.

Hikkomi-gaeshi (Fig 91a–e)

An attack which is very useful against an out-thrust left arm is this technique developed by Michael Borowski of East Germany – it is a variation of *hikkomi-gaeshi*.

Fig 91a   Gripping your opponent's left sleeve with your left hand and his left lapel with your right hand, drive his arm up in the air as if you were going to turn in for *seoi-nage*.

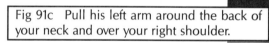

Fig 91b   Instead of turning in, duck your head under his arm and spread your feet.

Fig 91c   Pull his left arm around the back of your neck and over your right shoulder.

Fig 91d   Keeping tight contact, drop down to the floor into a hurdle stretch position, pulling down on his collar and arm and roll him over your shoulder.

Fig 91e Keep his arm pinned with both hands and as he lands be ready to roll on top into a *yoko-shiho-gatame*. It is important to drive strongly with the right leg to ensure that you break his balance in the first instance before dropping.

Seoi-nage on the 'wrong' side (Fig 92a–c)

A technique used by many Japanese shoulder throw specialists when confronted by a strong defensive left arm is to attack the 'wrong' way.

Fig 92a Taking an undergrasp on my opponent's left lapel with the right hand, my initial hold and stance suggests left *seoi-nage*.

Fig 92b By suddenly snatching the same lapel lower down with my left hand as well, I can attack unexpectedly with right *seoi-nage*.

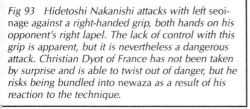

Fig 93 *Hidetoshi Nakanishi attacks with left seoi-nage against a right-handed grip, both hands on his opponent's right lapel. The lack of control with this grip is apparent, but it is nevertheless a dangerous attack. Christian Dyot of France has not been taken by surprise and is able to twist out of danger, but he risks being bundled into* newaza *as a result of his reaction to the technique.*

Fig 92c This can be very disconcerting for the opponent. Control is limited, but by getting well underneath and springing up with the legs it is possible to get your opponent high enough to score well, or at the very least, to make him sprawl on his front and go into groundwork with the advantage. The 1989 under-71kg World Champion, Koga of Japan, has had phenomenal success with this and similar techniques throughout his career and has such good control that he frequently scores ippon while holding on with just one hand.

Special trick techniques

These are specialist methods evolved by top competitors to counter problems they have encountered with particular opponents who proved difficult to grip and throw. Some may seem obvious once learned, but were unknown until someone devised them. The ability to create or at least pick up something new is one most champions seem to share.

Sugai's uchimata (Fig 94a–d)

A technique developed by Hitoshi Sugai of Japan for attacking with just a sleeve grip.

Fig 94a (Detail.) My opponent feels in danger because I have a good grip of his right sleeve with my left hand. He, in turn, is controlling my right sleeve to prevent me from getting a usable grip.

Fig 94b I cannot grip with my right hand because of his strong sleeve control.

Fig 94c Instead, I just give a strong left-hand pull and turn, throwing my right arm over the top as I do so.

Fig 94d As I lift my opponent with *uchimata* I grab whatever is available, normally his right elbow. This is a useful technique for making an attack when your opponent thinks he has you safely under control.

Yoko-gake as performed by Sekine (Fig 95a–d)

The undergrasp is by no means the preferred grip for all techniques.

Fig 95a This version of *yoko-gake* was developed by Shinobu Sekine of Japan. Against a left-handed fighter I grip right-handed with an overgrasp.

Fig 95b I quickly transfer my grip to a grip on the back of my opponent's collar with the fingers inside and step behind him with my right foot.

Fig 95c I hook my foot around his left ankle, pinning his weight on his left leg.

Fig 95d I jump behind him with my left foot, hanging on the back of his jacket all the time. I simultaneously hook his left foot away with my right leg and drive back with the left, pulling his upper body strongly to the floor as I fall with him.

Hikage's kansetsu-waza
(Fig 96a–c)

This technique for dealing with a strong defensive arm was devised by Nobutoshi Hikage, the under-78kg World Champion in 1983 and 1985.

Fig 96a   Faced with a strong defensive left arm, I grip under it to hold on to my opponent's left lapel with my right arm, and grip the end of his sleeve with my left hand.

Fig 96b   I step across in front of him with my right foot and throw the left foot behind as I pull his left sleeve over my right arm.

Fig 96c   I enter for a deep, stabbing attack with *seoi-nage*, but then I switch from attempting to throw him to forcing a submission by applying a straight armlock, pulling on the end of his sleeve and trapping his elbow against my chest.

Gripping Strategies

An old judo maxim is 'Know your opponent and know yourself'. One of the most striking examples of this in the entire history of judo occurred when Hitoshi Saito stepped on to the mat for the final of the World Heavyweight Championships in 1985 in Seoul, South Korea. Saito was reigning All-Japan and Olympic Champion and, having thrown all of his opponents for ippon with unstoppable *uchimata* and *osoto-gari* attacks, he looked set to follow in the footsteps of the recently retired Yamashita and to assert himself as an unbeatable champion. His opponent in the final, Jung-Chul Cho of South Korea, was a good 30kg (65lb) lighter and had struggled to reach the final, but unbeknown to everyone there he had spotted Saito's weak point and was ready to exploit it.

The 140kg (300lb) Japanese was all but unthrowable and had powerful *newaza*. Cho, however, saw one chance to win with an armlock attack and he took it. In the opening moments of the final, Saito, perhaps over-confident of his own abilities and under-estimating those of his opponent, reached out in a leisurely fashion with his left hand to take his favourite lapel grip hold. Cho grabbed his outstretched arm with both hands and slapped on a vicious but legitimate *waki-gatame*, forcing the Japanese to the ground. After a frantic struggle, Saito only just managed to extricate his arm. When both men stood up to continue the fight, it transpired that Saito's arm had been dislocated by the attack and he was forced to retire, conceding the contest to Cho. This was the most graphic example I had ever seen, in over twenty years in judo, of incisive gripping. Cho knew he had no chance against Saito who was then at the peak of his powers. So rather than grip up in the conventional way he went straight for the Japanese fighter's only weakness – his overconfidence

Fig 97 *The forward threat is so strong that the sudden switch back unbalances even very strong people. Note the independent hand action. From the threat of* yama-arashi, *pull changes to push and the left hand catches the Finn behind the knee to score* waza-ari.

– and snapped on the armlock as he reached out to take hold. This was not just an inspired bit of opportunism, it was something the Korean had planned and worked on and it came off brilliantly.

Gripping strategies rarely come off so com-

pletely or so perfectly but that contest, fough for the highest stakes, illustrates the impo tance of being able to analyse and anticipat your opponent's intentions.

The beauty of the orthodox sleeve and lape grips is that they are equally useful for bot attack and defence. This is not so true of man of the more modern variations – grips wher the arm goes over the opponent's shoulder t grip the belt. Some are, however, particularl inappropriate as defensive grips. Pulling a opponent into a bent-over position to grip hi

Fig 99 *Ude-gatame, the straight armlock, can be a useful technique against strong grippers who try to keep an attacking player out by stiff-arming. Preceded by a feint attack to the rear, such as* kouchi-gari, *in order to elicit a defensive reaction, it can succeed spectacularly. At the very least it is a useful gambit for opening up a defensive player. Here Ray Stevens puts Mariano Paduanno of Italy under serious pressure.*

Fig 98 *Peter Seisenbacher versus Janos Gyani: a good example of a one-handed attack, safe and tactically useful. The free hand can come into play to exploit the opponent's reaction to the threat of* kouchi-gari *by grabbing the leg when he moves it.*

belt and then attack is perfectly valid an effective in many cases, but the attack has t be immediate otherwise there is a stron possibility of a leg grab counter. The mor conventional high collar grip is also defen sively weak unless the arm gripping the colla is kept bent, ensuring continued control of th opponent's head and preventing a sudde armlock attack.

Another consideration that has to be taken into account is that many of the unorthodox grips that work so successfully in attack are actually prohibited by the rules from being used specifically for defensive purposes. If you grip your opponent's belt you must quickly attack or risk being penalised for non-combativity.

Changing grips and making repeated attacks in order to break up an opponent's rhythm and to prevent him getting his preferred grip or making a major attack himself is a defensive tactic which the rules currently permit.

Drag-down attacks using drop *seoi-nage* or *tomoe-nage* tend to be quickly penalised. The safest grips tend to be those which allow one-handed, minor-risk attacks, although the relative security of trying particular techniques is very much determined by whom you are fighting. Dave Starbrook lost an Olympic gold medal when he put in an *ouchi-gari* 'safety' attack on Shota Chochoshvilli in the 1972 Munich Olympic final because of the Russian's expertise with *uranage*.

The strong defence of Chris Bowles of Britain won him a Junior European gold medal in East Berlin in 1977, when he squashed his French opponent's successive attacks with drop *seoi-nage*. The Frenchman had thrown all his previous opponents for ippon with the technique so it obviously worked, but because of the rules he was actually disqualified for negative judo! It was the first time I had ever seen anyone disqualified for trying to throw his opponent!

It is very important to know how to grip and throw, but it can be equally important, if you are winning a contest, to be able to grip and control your opponent – primarily to prevent him from throwing you. Paul Radburn of Britain lost a bronze medal in the Moscow Olympics because he could only do one kind of judo – all out go-for-the-ippon, attacking, pressure judo – which made him a pleasure to watch, so long as he could keep it up. In his contest with Kockman of Czechoslovakia for the bronze medal he started out blitzkrieging his much heavier opponent, scoring *waza-ari*, *yuko* and *koka*. The big Czech though took his measure and closed up the gaps in his defence and Radburn then began to tire, but was unable to change his style; he could not just hang on and keep out of trouble. He was eventually thrown for ippon with *uchimata* only seconds away from an Olympic bronze.

His style may have been the direct result of his training. He was generally so much more physically powerful and aggressive than the majority of his training partners that he had not practised enough with the calibre of fighter who could put him under the kind of pressure required to make him learn defensive gripping and survival judo.

Two basic things that must be studied are how to impose your grip and how to break or negate your opponent's grip; if you are incapable of doing one or the other, at some point it will cost you a contest. Study the techniques presented in this chapter and above all practise them, particularly in *uchi-komi* and *nage-komi* situations.

Preventing grips

Preventing an opponent from taking his favourite grip can be all important, particularly at the start of a bout.

Defending the lapels (Fig 100a–c)

Fig 100a and b   One simple method to stop him taking a lapel grip is to use your own hand to grip the lapel where you sense he wants to take his grip.

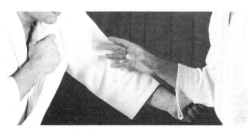

Fig 100c   Gripping your own lapel to stop your opponent from getting his grip does not preclude you from taking your grip as he searches for a hold.

Sleeve defence 1 (Fig 101)

Fig 101 There are a number of ways o preventing your opponent from getting a grip on your sleeve. Simply bending the arm tightens the jacket around the elbow join sufficiently to make it very difficult for him to retain his grip.

Sleeve defence 2 (Fig 102a and b)

Fig 102a and b   As you go to grip it is possible to slip your sleeve up your forearm and bend the arm to make it more difficult for your opponent to get a grip.

Blocking grips

Controlling the leading hand (Fig 103)

Fig 103 Often it is easier to prevent an opponent from taking a grip than it is to break free once you allow him to take a hold. An important drill to practise is catching his hand or wrist before he gets a grip and redirecting it. This can also be done by gripping the back of the elbow.

Blocking the high grip (Fig 104a and b)

Fig 104a and b Taller opponents may like to take a high collar hold, which can be extremely difficult to break once obtained. Prevent them from getting their grip by blocking the attacking hand. The forearm (Fig 104a) or elbow (Fig 104b) can be used to block their attempts to grip. If necessary step back to get out of reach.

Breaking grips

Breaking the lapel grip 1
(Fig105a–c)

If your opponent manages to get hold of your lapel, it can be quite difficult to break his grip. Usually it is necessary to use two hands against one plus the twisting power of the body.

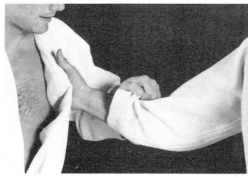

Fig 105a   In this method, the left hand grip the top of your opponent's sleeve.

Fig 105b   The right hands grabs his wrist.

Fig 105c   Push hard with both hands and at the same time step back forcefully to break his grip. Use your back to generate force.

Breaking the lapel grip 2
(Fig 106a and b)

Fig 106a   With this technique, the right hand grips your own left lapel (the one he is holding) and the left hand grips his sleeve.

Fig 106b   Push the sleeve hard down as you twist your upper body and pull on your own lapel to make him release his hold.

Breaking the lapel grip 3
(Fig 107a and b)

Another method of breaking an opponent's lapel grip.

Fig 107a   Grab the elbow of his judogi with the left hand and his wrist with the right.

Fig 107b   Give a sharp tug against the arm and jerk your body backwards, to break his grip.

Breaking the inside overgrasp
(Fig 108a and b)

Fig 108a and b   If an opponent attempts to bear down on your front defensive arm, simply drop your hand to the level of his hip, which will allow you to feel and control any attempts to attack. This is primarily and recognisably a defensive grip which should only be taken momentarily. Maintaining this grip excessively will get you penalised for non-combativity in contest.

Defensive grips

Cross grip defence (Fig 109a–c)

Fig 109a Your opponent has two hands on in a powerful high collar grip and is ready to attack.

Fig 109b He attempts a forward throw. Drop your left hand to block his hip and prevent him coming in. Transfer your right hand to a cross lapel grip.

Fig 109c Twist powerfully at the waist to pull your left hand free. Push him away with your right arm as you pull his right hand off. Look for the opportunity to do *yama-arashi* as he tries to regrip and reaches with his right hand.

Controlling the head (Fig 110)

Fig 110 As well as being a good principle of attacking judo, a high collar hold, controlling the opponent's head by pulling it into your chest and keeping your arm bent, makes it very difficult for him to attack you – it can therefore be useful as a defensive grip.

Controlling the biceps (Fig 111a and b)

Fig 111a and b Another useful principle of defensive gripping is to control the biceps. As your opponent grips your lapel or collar with his left hand (Fig 111a) grip his arm at the biceps with an open hand (Fig 111b). This provides remarkable control over him and can effectively negate any attempt to turn in for a left-handed technique. Of course, there is still danger from right-handed techniques and *ashi-waza*, but this grip can kill major forward throws like *tai-otoshi* or *harai-goshi* very effectively.

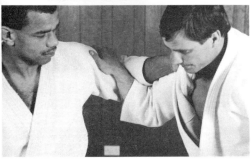

Fig 111a and 111b

Breaking a sleeve grip (Fig 112a–c)

Obviously the best way to prevent your opponent from getting a grip on the end of your sleeve is by moving and keeping the arm out of his way.

Fig 112a However, if he does get the end of your sleeve this is one among many other methods.

Fig 112b Try putting your left hand behind your knee and adding the power of your leg to the conflict.

Fig 112c Bend the knee and catch the back of your trouser leg with the gripped hand, then straighten it forcefully and it should break even the strongest grip.

Imposing your grip

Getting the sleeve (Fig 113a–c)

Getting the left hand on, or getting hold of your opponent's sleeve. Often it is not possible simply to grip as and where you like. Sometimes you have to be subtle.

Fig 113a One method for getting your left hand on an opponent's right sleeve in order to be able to attack with right-handed techniques is to grab it first with your right hand, reaching for it as if to shake hands.

Fig 113b Pull it across in front of you and you can easily transfer your grip from the right hand to the left.

Fig 113c Now you have his right sleeve safely gripped in your left hand.

Getting the lapel (Fig 114a–c)

Getting the right hand on, or getting a hold on your opponent's lapel.

Fig 114a Your opponent will not allow you to grab his left lapel with your right hand. Instead, grab the lapel near the belt with your left hand, which is a grip he will not find threatening.

Fig 114b Pull the jacket loose and you can easily pass his lapel into your right hand.

Fig 114c You now have your grip on his lapel with your right hand.

Getting the belt (Fig 115a–c)

Michel Nowak's method for getting his over-the-shoulder grip. The feeling of this sort of technique is a bit like climbing a tree.

Fig 115a   First the left hand cross grips the left lapel and pulls the opponent forwards, bending him off balance.

Fig 115b   The right hand is then thrown over the shoulder to grab the belt.

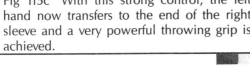

Fig 115c   With this strong control, the left hand now transfers to the end of the right sleeve and a very powerful throwing grip is achieved.

Getting the back grip (Fig 116a and b)

Fig 116a   When the leading arm is pulled across the body, the attacker does not always have to go for the belt.

Fig 116b   By gripping around the waist a similarly strong controlling effect can be achieved for *yoko-sutemi-waza*.

Gripping tricks

Getting the dominant sleeve grip (Fig 117a and b)

A canny way to get an attacking grip on the end of your opponent's sleeve and the stronger outer hand position.

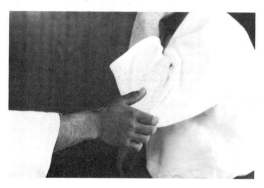

Fig 117a Bend your arm and offer him your sleeve in this bent position.

Fig 117b As he takes it, drop your hand over the top of his wrist and get the outside grip on his sleeve – simple but effective.

The slip (Fig 118a and b)

Fig 118a If an opponent gets a grip on your lapel which you find dangerous, disengage and, as you go to regrip, pull your jacket up higher by pulling down with the left hand and up with the right, sliding it around your neck.

Fig 118b As he takes his grip, release the tension with your left hand and pull down with the right. He will discover that he has gripped a lot lower than he had intended and you can get your grip with little trouble. A useful technique if you like standing armlocks.

Controlling the arm (Fig 119a–e)

Controlling the right arm in a right against right situation. This can be a defensive grip preventing your opponent from getting an attacking grip, but can also lead into attacks like the *seoi-nage* shown in Fig 119a–e. European Champion Pesniak of Russia was a master of this method and frequently scored with *osoto-gari* or *seoi-nage* off this grip.

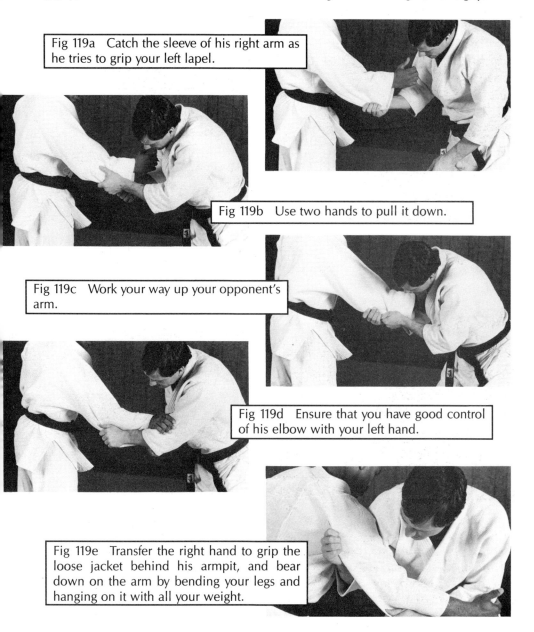

Fig 119a   Catch the sleeve of his right arm as he tries to grip your left lapel.

Fig 119b   Use two hands to pull it down.

Fig 119c   Work your way up your opponent's arm.

Fig 119d   Ensure that you have good control of his elbow with your left hand.

Fig 119e   Transfer the right hand to grip the loose jacket behind his armpit, and bear down on the arm by bending your legs and hanging on it with all your weight.

Blocking the lapel grip
(Fig 120a and b)

Fig 120a and b Here the forearm is being used to prevent an opponent from taking his grip. As your opponent goes to take his grip on your lapel, you can frustrate him if you already have your lapel grip by using your forearm to block down on his. This may cause him to make a rash attempt to grip if you persist, making him easier to throw.

Obtaining the undergrasp (Fig 121a–d)

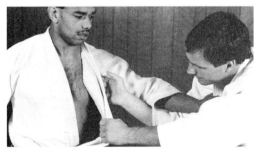

Fig 121a–d This is a useful trick for obtaining the undergrasp against a determined opponent. You have gripped his lapel with your right hand and he has taken the undergrasp with his left. Reach for his lapel with your left hand and pull it out slightly. Quickly pass your right arm over and under his left and grip just above where you are holding with the left hand – the undergrasp is now yours.

Illegal and banned grips (Figs 122–128)

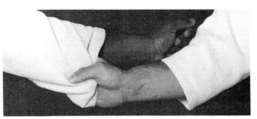

Fig 122 Gripping inside the sleeve with either the thumb or fingers is potentially injurious and consequently illegal.

Fig 123 Hooking the end of the sleeve was construed as a grip for defensive purposes and has been made illegal.

Fig 124 The reverse lapel grip so popular with Russian fighters, now illegal.

Fig 125 The ultra-defensive fingers in the belt and reverse lapel grip which makes it almost impossible to attack an experienced opponent, now illegal.

Fig 126 Gripping inside the cuff of the trouser leg: an illegal action.

Fig 128 Gripping the skirt of the jacket below the belt is considered a defensive grip and will be penalised in contest. However, once the jacket is pulled out of the belt, the skirt may be gripped if used to attack with immediately.

Fig 127 Gripping the end of the sleeve and screwing it up or twisting is an illegal action.

Illegal but ingenious (Fig 129a–e)

Fig 129a–e   This is a technique for gripping the end of an opponent's sleeve when you intend to break his grip and attack his forward arm. Putting the thumb in the cuff of the jacket is strictly speaking illegal, but it seems to me to be in the spirit of judo when confronted by a snug-fitting, tailored kit. Stick your left thumb in the end of your opponent's sleeve and pull it taut. Reach across with your right hand and the stretched cloth is easily gripped, however tight the jacket sleeve. Perhaps the rules should be modified to allow the inclusion and use of neat tricks like this one?

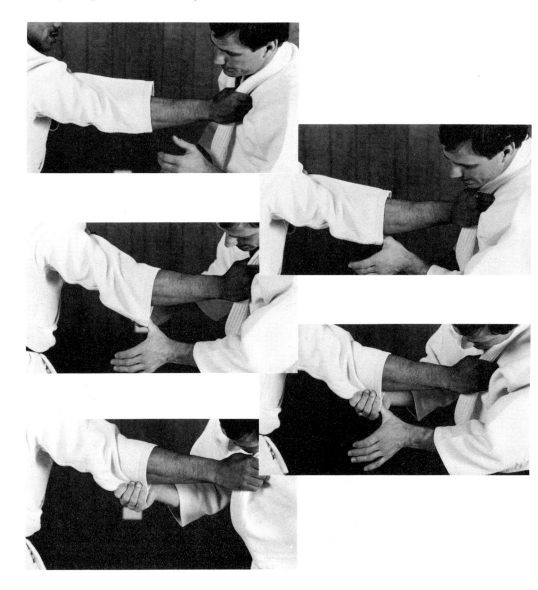

Developing Grip Strength

It is difficult for the average club player to imagine just how strong the top international fighters are and to what extent that strength is transmitted through the grip. In the 1979 World Championships in Paris, where I had won my first World bronze medal, I watched with interest the final of the open category between Sumio Endo of Japan and Vladimir Kusnetsov of the Soviet Union.

It was like watching judo from another epoch. The 39-year-old Russian had been brought out of a 10-year retirement and was a veritable bear of a man, standing 6ft tall and weighing over 130kg (290lb). Endo too was a superheavyweight at some 125kg (280lb), but he was only 5ft 6in tall and resembled nothing so much as a cannonball. Neither man moved around very much and there was only one clear attack in the whole contest, and that was made after the Russian had been penalised for non-combativity to *keikoku* and the Japanese

to *chui*. However, in the course of the contest, without turning in for any throws or going into *newaza*, the two men ripped apart four heavyweight double-weave judo jackets between them.

Although there was not much movement, it was apparent to the knowledgeable French crowd in the dusty old Coubertin stadium that they were witnessing a titanic struggle, and every time the referees penalised the two fighters for non-combativity they hooted their derision. When Endo did finally pick his moment and attack, he threw the mighty Russian for ippon with a brilliant *harai-makikomi* to become World Champion.

Few of us will ever need to develop the kind of power in the hands displayed by Endo and Kusnetsov, who were by no means alone in their predilection for tearing jackets on the international scene. But the importance of having grip strength that is effective to the

Fig 130 *The unorthodox gripping of Michel Nowak, though apparently scrappy, is very effective, allowing him to attack and build up a lead even though conditions are not perfect for scoring with an ippon throw. In spite of his opponent Fabien Canu having a good defence and dangerous throwing skills of his own, Nowak can attack almost with impunity.*

level at which you compete or practise is undeniable.

Training in judo will eventually develop a powerful grip; regular competition in particular will bring about increases in strength in the hands, wrists, forearms and shoulders. However, just as a marathon runner would not dream of attempting to run 26 miles without some preconditioning, no intelligent judo player should enter a contest without having done everything possible to prepare himself for the physical stresses and strains he is bound to encounter there.

For many players, the grip is the first thing to go in a contest. Watch any white-belt grading and you will almost inevitably see both fighters in agony after four minutes as a result of desperate gripping which pumps up the forearms with blood and lactic acid. Any beginner eager to feel what it will be like should go and hang from a bar for four minutes. That should give him some idea of why he ought to do exercises to strengthen the grip, and it is in fact quite a good way to develop grip strength in its own right.

The famous Belgian judo player Robert Van de Walle used to wrap a judo jacket around a chinning bar and do his chins and pull-ups

Fig 131   Densign White attacks Ray Stevens with seoi-nage. The high right-hand lapel hold and the lower grip on the left lapel allow White to attack left or right, making his intentions difficult to anticipate. Note the grip strength and muscle tone in the hands, wrists and forearms of top judo men.

to the back of the neck gripping the jacket – he thought it had more relevance effect to judo than gripping a bar.

Rope climbing is another favourite method in Japan and some top judo men are capable of remarkable gymnastic displays. Brian Jacks used to hang upside-down between two ropes with his feet pointing to the ceiling and his hands by his sides and pull himself to the top. He would pull until his arms were fully bent, then release his grip and quickly grab the ropes higher up before he fell. This would be repeated until he reached the top. Four times World Champion Shozo Fuji used to climb a rope one-handed without using his feet. Both men were, however, supremely gifted athletes and no one should attempt such feats without adequate supervision and a crash mat beneath them to prevent injury through falling.

The average judo player is best advised to begin by climbing using both arms and both legs, trapping the rope between the feet. (Climbing an 8m (25ft) rope five times is about the equivalent of doing five sets of ten chins in terms of effort expended.) As experience and strength increase try climbing one rope using hands only, then two ropes with one hand on each, before even considering any of the more exotic versions of the exercise.

Exercises for the grip can be performed as part of general body conditioning programmes. Exercises such as hanging leg raises and virtually all weight training using a bar has an incidental effect on the forearms. Particularly effective weight training exercises for the forearms include reverse curls, wrist curls, reverse curls keeping the wrists bent and the wrist roller. Even if you do not have access to a weight training gymnasium you can make a wrist roller yourself. All you need is a piece of broom handle about 25cm (10in) long, some clothes line and a brick or similar object, weighing from 5–10kg (10–20lb) depending upon how strong you are to start with. Rolling and unrolling the handle so that the weight is raised and lowered as the cord wraps and unwraps will soon have your forearms burning and your muscles will begin to grow very quickly indeed with this apparatus.

The exercises shown in the photographic sequences in this chapter are basic and need no special equipment. They are ideal as part of a warm-up for performing at the end of a session. They can also be particularly useful for childrens' classes as they can improve their grip strength with no danger of injury (as could happen if they were doing unsupervised weight training exercises).

Gripping exercises
(Figs 132–134)

Fig 132a and b   This is a good basic exercise for beginners and youngsters. You and your partner grab each other by the wrists and push and pull in a co-ordinated fashion, giving one another resistance as you do so. Alternate who grips on top and who grips underneath. Do sets of twenty.

Fig 133a and b   A similar exercise to the previous one, this time gripping one another's hands and hooking fingers in order to improve finger and grip strength.

Fig 134a and b   One of the most basic of exercises for strengthening the forearms, requiring no equipment or training partners. Stand with your arms outstretched and clench your fists. Quickly spring the hands open so that the palms stretch and quickly grip them closed again. Repeat for sets of fifty until the forearms are burning.

Fig 135   One unorthodox grip counters another in the 1985 under-78kg World Championship final. Hikage of Japan attempts to charge Denhmigen of East Germany to the mat with a leg grab as the German reaches for his belt. Denhmigen, though, counters his counter by grabbing his advanced left leg with his right hand and hooking his own left leg between Hikage's legs. The danger of grabbing the leg of a fighter who grips the belt is clear here, although Hikage was too strong to be caught like this.

Gripping Skills
and Self-Defence

The aim of practising judo is not to go looking for fights in order to prove how tough you are. Judo for me has always been a sport first and foremost – a competitive, dynamic combat sport – and not a way of guaranteeing success in back alley brawls or streetfights. While judo obviously has its uses in a real fight, to seek to use it for those ends ultimately cheapens and demeans it. People training in clubs should be aware that they will not be allowed to practise for very long if they make a habit of getting into trouble because they enjoy it.

Of course, there is a difference between looking for trouble and having it thrust upon you. The society we live in is far from perfect and self-defence is in fact the main reason most people take up judo. Keeping fit, however, does tend to be the main reason for continuing once reaching black belt – prob-ably because by then judoka have enough confidence in their physical abilities and are not excessively worried by the prospect of having to defend themselves.

In most cases the ability to defend yourself against an attacker by using judo depends upon your ability to grab hold of your assailant and throw him or her, or else armlock or strangle him or her. As has been stressed throughout this book, the grip is the pre-requisite to any throw. The importance of gripping skill for effective self-defence should not be underestimated, nor should your speed of reaction once you perceive the threat of attack. The well-trained judo player should be able to grab and throw in one movement – this can be trained for, although it is not perhaps as widespread as it ought to be.

There are many subtle variations of grips

Fig 136 Nobutoshi Hikage and myself, extreme
right versus extreme left. Hikage has taken a grip on
my hand and wrist to prevent me from taking my
sleeve and lapel grip, and he can push me back and
dominate as a result.

that can be applied to make self-defence
techniques more effective and, of course,
techniques have to be practised for those
eventualities when an attacker might not be
wearing a jacket. A man in a T-shirt is no
more difficult to throw than a man wearing a
jacket, it just requires a different approach.
Some techniques which work very well in
contest will not necessarily be ideal for self-
defence purposes. *Juji-gatame*, *uchimata* and
drop-knee *seoi-nage* immediately spring to
mind as examples of the kind of skills best
reserved for the dojo. There is as much chance
of inflicting severe damage on yourself as
there is on your attacker with such techniques.
Osoto-gari, *kube-nage*, *tai-otoshi* and most of
the *ashiwaza* are better bets altogether.

An additional consequence of being a
skilled grip fighter is that your hand speed
improves significantly over that of an un-
trained person and you become quite good at
catching hands, wrists and arms. This can be
very good training for blocking the punches,
swings and clawing attempts that characterise
the typical street attack. Skills developed from
practising leg grabs come in very handy when
someone tries to kick you and, of course, competition judo makes you aware of the dangers
of a head-butt.

Breaking grips on the wrist (Fig 137a–c)

Fig 137a–c Breaking an opponent's grip on your wrist is very simple. Just turn the gripped wrist by bending your arm at the elbow and making a circular motion so that pressure is applied to his thumb. If he takes a reversed grip it is even easier than if he takes a standard hold.

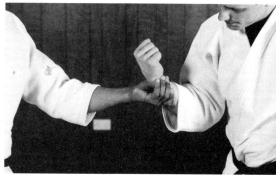

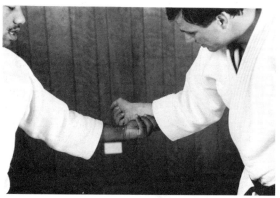

Afterword

In a sense this part of the book is probably the hardest to write. I have always been an attacking player with a positive outlook and have gone into all of my contests looking for the ippon throw or groundwork move. I never liked to dwell on defeats, but I believe you have to analyse what went wrong in those contests you lose in order to learn from your mistakes and do better next time.

Khabarelli is a fighter who gave me great difficulty and whose style is burned into my memory. He was right-handed with a non-stop aggressive attacking style that made me feel passive even when I beat him. His fitness was superb and he never stopped coming for me throughout each one of our contests – these were each among the longest five minutes of my life. Every time we fought I spent my time trying to stop him getting his arm over my shoulder and gripping my belt at the back. After each contest I came off feeling

as if I had just been in a fight with a wild animal of some kind; I was delighted when he moved up from the under-71kg category to the under-78kg category for the Moscow Olympics, although I was soon to follow myself.

Michel Nowak of France was always a similar sort of proposition, although I never lost to him as I did to the Russian whose technical scope was much wider. Michel Nowak's approach to contest was exactly the same, but he never sustained it until the last minute. In his case it was a question of concentrating and surviving four minutes of pressure. This was not because he was not fit; he simply had a different physiological make up to Khabarelli – probably a higher concentration of white fast twitch muscle fibres, which would also explain why he was so formidably strong. I fought him seven times, never lost and hated every contest I had with him. My best performance was a *waza-ari* win in 1984 when I caught him with a footsweep in the European Championships.

I remember Nobutoshi Hikage as being exceptionally strong and very skilful, especially at *kumikata*. He was not the most technical Japanese I had ever fought in contest, but definitely the strongest. He was a very dangerous thrower with strong *newaza* and no real weaknesses that I could find to exploit. He liked *tani-otoshi*, left *harai-goshi* and *ashiwaza*. Worst of all he was very hard to attack without putting yourself in danger of being countered or dragged to the floor.

Our first meeting in the final of the World Championships in 1983 was really close and I felt I had done enough to win. In the second encounter, which was in the first round of the Seoul Olympics in South Korea, he was even stronger and never let me get going, killing my grip and pushing me back all the time. He clearly dominated me and that day was to be the first time I ever won a medal in a major event without actually scoring on anyone. As with Miguel in Seoul in 1988, I took every contest after losing to Hikage by skin-of-the-teeth decisions; it was determination and skill in gripping that won me that bronze medal.

Enzio Gamba of Italy was another left-hander who gave me considerable problems; I thought he was a brilliantly skilful judo man with a good tactical fighting brain. His superb gripping negated a lot of my advantages in terms of range of throws in the 1980 Olympic final when he prevented me taking the gold medal. Frank Wienecke turned out to be my other Olympic nemesis in 1984 in Los Angeles. Analysing the video afterwards it seemed to me that I was clearly winning when I relaxed a little bit too much and gave him the scope to begin his judo. It cost me a gold medal when he produced his now famous right *uchimata*, left *seoi-nage* combination out of the blue. I had nightmares about that final for months afterwards. Sometimes I think I was slightly a victim of being too good at killing people's techniques with superior gripping, not even letting the danger begin. As a consequence, on those rare occasions when I did get caught, I had less chance of recovering than those people who were more frequently on the receiving end, but that's life I suppose!

At the end of the day everyone has weaknesses and it is the opposition's job to find out where they are and to try to exploit them. That is one very compelling aspect in the fascinating study of judo. For a long time in Britain the weakness has been in *kumikata*, but times are changing – hopefully this book will help to accelerate that change.

Appendix

he day of the closely-fitting, tailored jacket in
nternational competition is, for the moment at
east, over. At the beginning of 1990, the Inter-
ational Judo Federation introduced an amend-
nent to the existing rules to enforce a larger
acket, returning to the look of former years.

Of course, this was not done for cosmetic
easons. Tight jackets inhibit the opponent's
rip and promote defensive gripping tactics.
irip breaking was increasingly a strong
eature of competitions from the middle of the
970s through to the end of the 1980s.

Japanese influence pushed through the
hange in the rules in the hope that a looser
acket would prevent judo becoming like
vrestling, and would promote more impressive
nd dramatic throws. The new rule principally
ffects the size of the sleeve. The rule states:

he contestants shall wear judogi (Judo
niform) complying with the following con-
litions:

a) Strongly made in cotton or similar
   material, in good condition (without rent
   or tear).

b) White or off-white in colour.

(c) Acceptable markings:
   (i)   Control number (on back of jacket).
   (ii) National emblem (on left breast of
         jacket). Maximum size 100cm^2.
   (iii) Manufacturer's trade mark (on bottom-
         front of jacket). Maximum size 25cm^2.
   (iv) Shoulder markings (from the collar
         across the shoulders down the arms
         and on both sides of jacket). Maximum
         length 25cm and maximum width
         5cm.
   (v)   The contestant's name may be worn
         on the belt.

(d) The jacket shall be long enough to cover
    the thighs and shall have a minimum reach
    to the fists when the arms are fully ex-
    tended downwards at the sides of the body.
    The body of the jacket shall be wide
    enough to cross over at the level of the
    bottom of the rib-cage with a minimum
    overlap of 20cm.

    The sleeves of the jacket must reach to
    the wrist-joint as a maximum and 5cm
    above the wrist-joint as a minimum.

    A space of 10–15cm shall exist between
    the sleeve and the arm (inclusive of band-
    ages), on the entire length of the sleeve.

Index